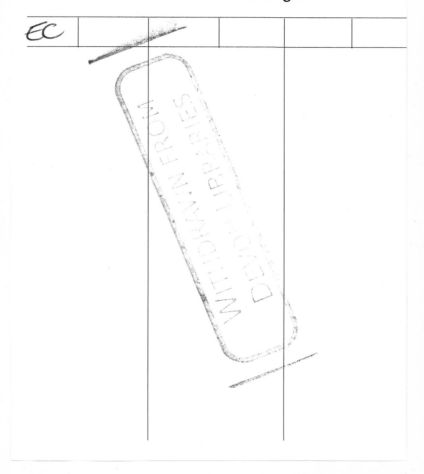

TWO
MARGARINES
AND OTHER DOMESTIC DILEMMAS!

JOHN SHUTTLEWORTH'S
GUIDE TO EVERYDAY LIFE

OMNIBUS PRESS

Cover designed by Paul Tippett

ISBN: 978-1-787-60062-1

Image credits

Alan Clift: p. 4; Lucy Day: front cover, p. 11, p. 42, p. 57, p. 166, p. 180,
p. 232, p. 239, p. 253, p. 272, p. 279; Derek Fellows: p. 174; Kathryn
Heywood: p. 23, p. 82, p. 100, p. 114, p. 129, p. 160, p. 183; Tony Briggs:
back cover.

Printed in the Czech Republic

A catalogue record for this book is available from the British Library.

CONTENTS

INTRODUCTION

Hello, yes... erm... well, if this is the introduction, which the subtitle suggests it is, I suppose I'd better introduce myself. But do I need to? If you look at the spine of the book you'll find out exactly who I am. John Shuttleworth it says, and it's true, that is my name. I'm a versatile singer/organist. I live in Sheffield, South Yorkshire and I drive an Austin Ambassador (Y reg). Why? I'll tell you later! I reside in a very nice semi-detached house with my charming wife Mary (a dinner lady at a local primary school) and our West Highland terrier, Kirsty, although for years I've been calling her a Scottie dog, which is very silly of me as it's a different breed entirely. Again, more of that later...

Mary and I have two children, Darren and Karen, who are fully grown now, to the extent that Karen left home a couple of years ago and lives in Mansfield where she's a nursery assistant. As for Darren, he still lives at home and is also an assistant — assistant manager at Bargain Booze. He used to work for Victoria Wine, which was taken over by Augustus Barnet, but sadly Augustus decided to sell it and now it's just Bargain Booze, which obviously doesn't sound as grand as Augustus Barnet, but it can't be helped. For a short while Darren lived in a bedsit with his friend Plonker. His real name is 'Lee', but he prefers to be called 'Plonker', which you'd think would hold him back in life, and to be honest, I think it has, as he's a bit aimless and currently unemployed. Mind you, so am I (unemployed, that is – I'm certainly not aimless!). I used to work for Comet, demonstrating audio equipment, and before that I was a security guard for a sweet factory in the Rotherham area. Obviously, I can't say exactly where, for security reasons.

John's Explanatory Note: I've just remembered that Karen used to have a rabbit, but it died of natural causes a good few years ago. The rabbit hutch wasn't empty for long though as Plonker started storing a reconditioned car engine in it for his Datsun Sunny. So could you argue that Karen's rabbit died in order to breathe new life into Plonker's motor? Well, you could argue that, I suppose, but it's a very fanciful idea, and most ordinary people would think you were a bit barmy saying that, as would I.

I live next door to a single gent who has played a very important role in my life, and that's because as well as being my next-door neighbour and a dear friend, Ken Worthington is my sole agent – you know, he gets me bookings to sing and play my organ at the drop-in centre or the halfway house, and occasionally the St John's Ambulance Rooms. In addition, when travel to and from venues is required – Ken negotiates my petrol money. Sometimes Ken even gets me a fee, but that's a rare occurrence these days, to be honest. It's a shame because before I met Ken I played 'Wishee Washee' in Aladdin at the Dinnington Alhambra '3rd blockbusting year!' – it said on my publicity photo. That was a long time ago now. I was also an Ethiopian slave in Aida – that was only amateur but it was at the Crucible Theatre, Sheffield. (You know, where they put the snooker on – fantastic!)

Older readers may remember Ken as 'TV's Clarinet Man' when he made a disastrous appearance on *New Faces* in 1973 (more of that later, as well!). In fact – more of everything (especially brackets, which I love) (Why, don't YOU? I thought everybody did...). Ken lives in a bungalow whereas we – the Shuttleworth family – live in a semi-detached house (as I've already stated), which of course has stairs to negotiate. Ken has no stairs whatsoever, though he does have a nice pair of stepladders which he rarely uses, but I frequently borrow. Thanks for the lend, Ken!

––––––––––––––

John's Explanatory Note: I know Ken will receive that thank-you message because he has kindly agreed to proofread this book upon its completion. Ken's vast experience in the entertainment industry will no doubt be used in a wily way to make improvements to the manuscript, to help make it a massive best-seller. Ooh, I do hope so, I'm very excited! But right now, erm... I'd better calm down and crack on with the intro.

––––––––––––––

A low boundary wall divides the two properties (our house and Ken's bungalow), and occasionally the fabric of the wall is threatened by Ken walking along the top of it in his Cuban heels, usually while he consumes a bowl of Cheerios. "Why not Sultana Bran or Crunchy Nut Cornflakes?" I hear you asking. I really don't know – you'd have to ask Ken that question yourself, if you ever meet him, which is unlikely as, ever since his humiliation on *New Faces*, Ken has shunned the limelight and goes bright red in social situations.

Having said that, Ken is a very stylish dresser. Besides his Cubans, I've seen him wear tailored shirts with lots of buttons on and he's got a silk bomber jacket with the word 'Whitesnake' emblazoned on the back, which I was wary of initially, but now I accept it, as I do his leather bomber jacket which has two large zips at the front (similar to the one Lovejoy used to sport – do you

These are NOT Ken's stepladders, incidentally. I bought this pair from Barry MacMahon for £3 in 1982. They are now rather rickety, and for occasional use only!

remember?). Many a time I've watched Ken struggle to do those zips up, but I've never offered to help him – I hope you don't think that's mean of me? Now, you'll like this... Ken claims he used to be a beatnik, and once owned a finger monkey! Hmm... I don't know if I believe that, do you, readers? It does seem a bit unlikely, but that's what Ken claims, and it's something else to ask him if you ever DO meet him!

I like to get up nice and early of a morning, generally before my wife, Mary, who works as a dinner lady at a local primary school. Ooh, I've said that already, haven't I? Apologies... still, it bears repeating, and what I didn't say before but I will now is that Mary is on 'mixed veg', which is a crucial central position as a dinner lady. Her friend and work colleague, Joan Chitty, who might be popping round later, used to be on 'custard', but now her job is to break up scuffles in the dinner queue. Well, anticipate them, ideally – that's the dream. Joan used to drive a Mini Metro, but recently has taken possession of a Citroen Berlingo, and I'm quite envious, I must say, as they've got eye-level storage units within the main body of the vehicle. Mind you, my Austin Ambassador has a fantastic glove compartment, and when you open it, my travel sweets (generally Werther's Originals but I do like to rotate them with a quality barley sugar) slide down to within easy access of an outstretched hand. The left one, obviously!

During school holidays Mary does seem to enjoy a lie-in, I must say, but she might not like me mentioning that so I'd appreciate it if you'd forget what I've just said. Erm, what else can I say about my wife? Well... her hairdo is to some extent the shape of a motorcycle helmet. (Oof, she won't like me mentioning that either, but it's important that I do). By the way, I'm referring to the old-fashioned helmet, not the full-face one with a visor as that would imply a big floppy fringe right over her face, like that lad from the Flock of Seagulls – remember them? They've gone a bit quiet, as have a lot of bands from the eighties. And the seventies, not to mention the sixties. You don't hear much of Freddie and the Dreamers these days, do you? Or the fun combo Racey, who – Ken tells me – hail from the West Country – what are they up to, I wonder? And what about Modern Romance, who always had lovely crisp white shirts (ironed presumably by their mothers?).

But back to Mary's hairdo. Years ago, when we were courting, Mary worked at the post office – not as a sub-postmistress, I must stress. Her job was to put boxes of rubber bands and drawing pins on the shelves, and, erm... Jiffy bags? Ooh no, I'm not sure they were around back then. But envelopes, certainly. I believe they had a sweets section too, so Mary would have handled Aztecs and Jameson's Ruffle Bars, etc. Fantastic! Anyway, I used to pick up Mary after work on the Honda 70 (I couldn't afford a car back then, and certainly not an Austin Ambassador Y reg!).

John's Explanatory Note: Readers may be interested to learn that I had two tartan pannier bags affixed to the, erm... panniers of my Honda 70, which would rattle noisily whenever I went over a bump in the road, especially if I forgot to do up the buckles, which frequently I did.

As I was saying, I used to pick Mary up from the post office, after work, and one evening as I arrived it was getting dark (so it must have been winter time), and I couldn't see very well, and when Mary got onto my Honda 70, I started to drive off straight away. She shouted "Wait, wait! I haven't got my helmet on!" But I thought she had, you see, because of the shape of her hairdo. That's the end of that little story, which I told at our wedding. It went down very badly (with Mary, anyway!).

Occasionally, Mary's hair is not like a motorcycle helmet at all. Once – I think it was possibly in 2004 – I recall Mary waking up with wild hair a bit like a member of Hot Gossip. Do you remember that pop dance combo? They've gone quiet, an' all. They never seemed to stand up, did they, preferring to crawl along the TV studio floor, which you'd have thought was a sure-fire way to ladder your tights. But they often had dishevelled hair as if they'd been crawling through bushes. Mary would never do that, but the previous night she had visited a public house in the local vicinity with Joan Chitty, and at some point in the evening, Joan had sprayed some hairspray in Mary's hair, and it was still in there next morning. Anyway, Mary looked quite different with this wild Hot Gossipy hair — a bit raunchy, you know. She looked in the mirror and was quite shocked, but she soon combed it out back to her normal 'motorcycle helmet' style and went downstairs to wipe the kitchen surfaces, but I was a bit sad because I quite liked it. Having said that, I do accept that it wasn't a suitable style for a mature married lady to sport on a regular basis.

Mary doesn't snore, I'm happy to reveal, though a few weeks ago I was woken up in the middle of the night by what sounded like a fox barking, a plaintive distant sound that I couldn't immediately locate. It was very regular rhythmic barking, about once every three seconds. I assumed it was a young vixen raiding the bins in the big old house across the road, which is occupied by some arty student types who keep strange hours, and they tend to let their bins overflow. Anyway, I listened with bated breath to this fox. Presumably she was calling to her mate to inform him there were remnants of a Pot Noodle on offer. I decided to get out of bed and go outside with my torch, which has a powerful beam and three modes, including two flashing at different speeds — useful surely to confuse and scare off even the wiliest of foxes! But before I could get up, I realised the fox noise seemed to be emanating not from outside but from INSIDE the bedroom — in fact, right next to me — coming out of Mary's nose! Surely not? Could there be a little fox in her nose, I briefly wondered?

I cocked my head to one side and positioned my ear close to Mary's nose (not a nice thing to do to a spouse at the best of times, I realise, and especially not when they're asleep!), but it was essential for me to grasp the full situation. Just then Mary woke up and gasped, "What the hell are you doing, John?" I didn't reply, but kept my ear cocked above Mary's nose and continued to listen, and interestingly – the fox had stopped barking!

Can you guess what was going on here, readers? Well, I'll tell you – there wasn't a fox outside the house at all! No, but a regular raspy noise was being produced in Mary's nose which sounded just like a fox barking each time she breathed out (or in, I'm not sure which). Now she was awake the fox noise had of course stopped, although Mary's nose then started producing a snorting noise (of disbelief) when I told her what she'd been doing.

We've laughed about that incident on numerous occasions since. Well, I have – Mary gets cross whenever I mention it, and still denies that she was the producer of the fox sound, so my laughter has to be subdued when discussing it. In fact, it's no fun mentioning it any more as Mary can become quite unpleasant about it, so this is probably the last time I will mention it to anyone.

I digress, but to be honest that will happen a lot in this book, readers, so please get used to it. Also, each chapter will contain a host of domestic dilemmas that we'll need to tackle, because that's the purpose of this book after all, and – let's face it, domestic dilemmas occur continually throughout the day and we have to be ready to deal with them as they pop up. Once you have the solution to each dilemma, Life will become that little bit easier. Not too easy though – Life isn't meant to be a complete doddle, you know!

CHAPTER 1:

THE DELICATE ART OF OPENING
THE CURTAINS

Hello, it's me again – John Shuttleworth. I'm glad you lasted beyond the introduction. Now, every morning I get out of bed and open the curtains, but only slightly or Mary might wake up and shout "Too bright!" If that happens I just reduce the gap to an amount acceptable to both her and me, and that can take a while. You see – I need to have enough light to locate my slippers and put on my dressing gown, but if it's too bright Mary will receive a rude awakening and become quite rude to me in return! So with this dilemma I suggest you remain quick to react and ever-sensitive to the other person's demands, without losing sight of your own, obviously. Grasp the curtain between finger and thumb while maintaining eye contact with the person in bed as you make small adjustments with the curtain, and don't smile or be too chatty, because they don't like that!

I recently wrote a song about this dilemma. I'll sing you a snatch of it, shall I? Oh yes, songs are something you'll be hearing a lot throughout this book to illustrate various dilemmas. I do like to perform them on my Yamaha organ with built-in auto accompaniment. Sometimes (if there's no power source handy and batteries have gone flat), I'll sing them without the organ – a cappella – as they have extremely honed lyrics, in my humble view. They also have very catchy tunes which, sadly, you'll have to imagine – unless you know them already, in which case you can sing along. Sing along anyway, with your own tune if you like – even if it's not very good!

OOH, SHE SAID

Each night I close my bedroom curtains
And I take great delight
In tucking them behind the radiator
I like to get it right
And in the morning I open them
But just a little at first
Or my wife tends to shout at me
And has been known to curse

"Ooh," she says – "that's too much
I'm still half asleep"
"Ooh," she says – "that's not enough
I can hardly see"
"Yes," she says – "that's just right
Now please let me be
Off you go and make me a cup of tea!"

And I do just that. Down to the kitchen I go to put the kettle on, but hang on… on the way downstairs another dilemma may present itself which we must deal with pronto!

Kirsty — looking a bit fed up. Maybe it's because that first song didn't mention her? She needn't worry — there's a lovely one all about her at the end of Chapter 17.

The welcome mat – what if it's slightly askew?

You straighten it up. There, that was simple, wasn't it! Not so much of a dilemma after all. But wait a sec – in order to justify the subtitle perhaps we should examine WHY the welcome mat was askew? Well, it wasn't me, I assure you, and our Scottie dog Kirsty is too small to move the heavy coir matting (with rubberised base) when she scampers with her paws. Karen isn't back at home on one of her occasional visits, so I suspect my son Darren must have dislodged it the night before on his way up to his bedroom. He would have had unsteady and erratic footwork as he tried to keep his cereal bowl steady while simultaneously mounting the stairs, and this is what may have moved the mat from its rightful place.

Now here's a thing: my next-door neighbour (and sole agent) Ken Worthington uses his welcome mat differently from the rest of us. You may find this mildly disturbing or you may take it in your stride, which I'd prefer you to, to be honest. Ken has a posher welcome mat than most of us. It doesn't just say 'Welcome'. Below the word 'Welcome' it says 'Goodbye', but written upside down. So as you come into your house you're supposed to see the word 'Welcome', and as you leave, the word 'Goodbye'.

Clever, you might think, but what Ken's done is to turn his mat the wrong way round so that when he leaves his house it says 'Welcome' as in 'Welcome World' (says Ken). When Ken returns home he's greeted with the word 'Goodbye' as in 'Goodbye World'. What a crazy thing to do, you may think, but you have to realise that Ken lives alone, so he has no one to welcome him or say goodbye to – it makes perfect sense to Ken. But not to a normal family man like myself, and I'm sure the mat's manufacturers would be horrified if they knew Ken was misusing their product in this way.

What about the lounge curtains?

Good point – before we start brewing tea we must open them, and unless Darren's friend Plonker is sleeping on the settee, which only happened once and hopefully won't ever again – the vintage car coasters had been scattered around the coffee table, and there was a discarded Oreos wrapper on the carpet! – all downstairs curtains must now be opened fully. Please take care if they're posh ones on a cord like a curtain for a stage where a play's about to start. Pull gently but firmly, knees bent, back slightly arched, and be ready to stop if you meet any resistance. If you do, investigate the problem before continuing with the task.

You may want to sit down momentarily to recover from being blinded by the bright daylight, and if so you are free now to polish your shoes, if you forgot to polish them the night before (naughty, naughty!). You might prefer to do that after you have enjoyed your first cup of tea but no... come on, do them now! And while you polish I shall spur you on with a jaunty song which should be sung raucously, as you might perform a slightly cheeky sea shanty!

A SHINY PAIR

I used to polish my shoes every day
"Remember the newspaper," Father would say
Firstly, I'd remove any dirt with a brush
This task was crucial and couldn't be rushed

Now I was ready to put polish to shoe
With a circular motion, and sparingly too
Then with a duster I would vigorously buff
Until my arm felt like it was dropping off

But for youngsters today
It's a different affair
Modern shoewear requires little care
They waltz round in trainers
With a nonchalant air
But they'll never know the thrill of
A shiny pair

Trainers, it's true
Are a low-maintenance shoe
Just wipe with a damp cloth and they're good as new
But for youngsters today
Is life such a hoot?
For they'll never know the joy of a gleaming boot

I used to polish my shoes every day
"Remember the newspaper," Father would say
I'll never forget the day I forgot
He gave me a clout and he called me a clot!

But for youngsters today
It's a different affair
Modern shoewear requires little care
They waltz round in trainers
With a nonchalant air
But they'll never know the thrill of
A shiny pair

Oof, you missed a bit! Only kidding – well done to all those who actually DID polish their shoes while they sang. YOU deserve a cup of tea! "What about the dilemmas in making a cup of tea then, John," you may be asking? Well, there aren't any, silly – you just put the kettle on and make a cup of tea! Caught you out there, didn't I!

John's Explanatory Note: Or did I? Keen domestic dilemma spotters may argue that while the kettle is boiling a host of dilemmas emerge: should you clean the worktop with a quality surface spray (prior to wiping down with a damp cloth); or should you be checking that the mug tree is vertical, and if not begin repositioning mugs to correct the angle? Or would your time be best spent emptying your toaster's crumb tray?

Ooh, I don't really know. Erm... you could instead just sit on your bar stool drumming your fingers on the worktop and listening to the different fascinating stages in the kettle's boiling process – the initial crack of expanded metal (more common in older-style kettles designed for heating on the gas hob), the whoosh as the water approaches boiling temperature, and – my favourite stage – that moment as the whoosh recedes and, after a moment of silence, a comforting bubbling sound is heard as the water boils. Please wait for the kettle's 'off' click before dispensing the water into cups or teapot, or the whistle, if it's an old-fashioned kettle. (And don't forget to turn off the hob!)

Should you ask other people in the building if they'd like a cup of tea as well? Well, yes, but what if you've only got one teabag left? Far better to assume that you thought they'd just had a cuppa. So hmm, yes, while there clearly are a few tea-making dilemmas, it's only once the tea has been made that the problems really start!

CHAPTER 2:

ONE CUP OF TEA IS NEVER ENOUGH (INCORPORATING MICROWAVE MISERY)

One of the most regular dilemmas you'll face in life is whether you should go for that second cup of tea. It's a dilemma that crops up several times every day if you're a tea drinker, unless you drink them funny herbal ones. Oof, there's no way anyone could drink more than one of those at a time, surely! Another song may help here.

ONE CUP OF TEA IS NEVER ENOUGH, BUT TWO IS ONE TOO MANY

I love a nice hot cuppa, it really satisfies me
Before I sip I tend to blow to cool the liquid slightly
I can't think of a drink that can so refresh me
But all too soon it's down my throat, and I'm staring at an empty

ONE CUP OF TEA IS NEVER ENOUGH

Time for a top-up − that all-important second cup
But after an initial sip, I lose interest in it
I'll dunk a biscuit − better not, I've had a few already
Suddenly my thirst has gone, and the mug is getting heavy

One cup of tea is never enough and two is one too many
One cup of tea is never enough and two is one too many
I've searched for answers to this conundrum, but I can't find any
One cup of tea is never enough and two is one too many

Oh, what an ass am I (*Assam − do you get it?*)
For two cups to crave
I'm heading for an early grave (*Early grave? Earl Grey − do you get that one, as well?*)

One cup of tea is never enough and two is one too many
One cup of tea is never enough and two is one too many
I've searched for answers to this conundrum, but I can't find any
One cup of tea is never enough and two is one too many

Is one cup of tea always never enough?

Before I answer that, I have to say that sometimes just one sip is more than enough. "Really John?" I hear you asking. "Can you elaborate?" Yes − I'm about to, if you give me a chance!

When one sip of tea is more than enough

This happens when you've accidentally picked up somebody else's cup of tea and it's incredibly sweet, or not sweet enough. You're going to gag on it, aren't you, or at least grimace, and put the cup down smartish. But don't overreact and spit out the brew all over your trousers − or your skirt, if you're a lady.

John's Explanatory Note: Or if you're undergoing the 'transfiguration', is it called? Our Karen says that's becoming quite common. Well, I wouldn't know, but I want my book to be inclusive, so yes, whatever you're wearing, including a kilt, shorts or leggings, which Mary frequently sports.

Please don't spit out yer tea, because that's dirty. So is chucking it into a flowerpot like in that coffee ad of yesteryear. "What do I do with the cup then?" Simple – you pass it back to the person you stole it from, and apologise profusely. Mind you, they probably won't want it back after you've been drinking it!

One sip is also more than enough when it's definitely your drink but you thought it was tea, and it's not – it's coffee! This may happen if you've been concentrating on doing a puzzle for hours and forgotten that it's coffee time and someone has kindly swapped your empty tea cup for a mug of coffee. The shock is monumental. Well, it's not that bad, but it's not pleasant. You were sure it was tea and it's not, it's coffee, so you go "Ugh!" or "Agh!" if you're really shocked. I can usually laugh about it a few seconds later, because nobody died – that's one way to look at it. Just pour it away and make yourself a tea, or if you don't want to anger your partner (who made you the hot drink with all good intentions), accept that it's coffee time, and that you shouldn't still be in your pyjamas now, anyway. Have a few sips and your taste buds will soon adjust.

Even more upsetting (again, usually when you're immersed in a puzzle), is when you absently reach for your last square of chocolate or second and final Twix finger, only to discover you've already eaten it and all that's left is the blinking wrapper! That's heart-breaking, that is.

John's Explanatory Note: When I mentioned that to Ken he joked that I should have eaten the second finger first, and then the problem might not have arisen. I said, "Very funny, Ken" – which it was, I think you'll agree. Well, relatively amusing. Not bad, for someone who came last on *New Faces* and is often shrouded in melancholy and feelings of low self-worth.

Are two cups of tea always one too many?

Well now, this answer may surprise you, but... No. First thing in the morning is a time when two or even three cups of tea can be downed with ease, and I often do. I know I've contradicted myself there and undermined my song by saying that, but it can't be helped. And now we come to our final tea dilemma!

What if your tea gets cold before you've finished drinking it?

If you get distracted by a puzzle? Yes, it could be, or a sudden movement in a bush in your garden, which you're worried might be an escapee from a local jail taking cover, although relax – it's probably just the wind getting up. Something that's happened that makes you forget about your tea, anyway...

When you finally come out of your reverie and remember you've got a cup of tea on the go, it may be stone cold and need reheating in the microwave. It sounds like a simple thing to do and not really a dilemma – you just get up and reheat it, surely? But oh ho ho, my friend, if only it was as simple as that!

Microwave misery

The first time you pop your cup of cold tea in to reheat, chances are you'll microwave it for insufficient time, so when it pings your tea's still only lukewarm. You'll have to microwave it again. But in your haste to retrieve your mug after the first reheating, you may have knocked the microwave plate off the plastic knobbly thing in the middle, so before you can reheat your tea a second time you will have to relocate the plate, and that could take a while, during which time your tea will have cooled even further, so do remember to add on a few seconds when you set the microwave timer.

However, not wishing to be caught out and to have to reheat it a third time, you may overcompensate and reheat for so long that your tea's now scalding hot and undrinkable. So, there's nothing for it but to sit back down with your overly hot tea (it might even be bubbling like a witch's cauldron!), and while you're waiting for it to cool, what happens?

You become distracted again by a puzzle?

No, not by a puzzle this time – I'm getting fed up of using that as an example and you must be tired of hearing it too, so let's say... by a leaflet for conservatories that's just come through the door? Ooh, fantastic! Well, whatever it is, you're distracted and your tea's going to get cold again, and so you'll have to reheat it yet again, and this vicious cycle could repeat many, many times during the day.

Drinking tea while having a cuddle

Well, in a nutshell, they don't go together. I remember one evening – it was 2010 or possibly 2011. My wife Mary was in the lounge watching telly and I came to join her carrying a mug of tea that I'd already reheated several times. I'd been adjusting the action on the front gate, you see, and kept popping out to check it, meaning my tea remained undrunk. Finally – job completed – I reheated my tea, knowing this time I'd have the opportunity to sit down and drink it hot, to the dregs. However, Mary was in a strange mood, saying she'd like a cuddle (I think she'd been watching an emotional episode of *Doc Martin*), so I left my armchair and joined her on the settee.

Did I forget to bring my tea? No fear, it came with me and I placed it on a coaster on the coffee table. But putting my arms round Mary to give her a cuddle meant my hands were no longer free, so I couldn't take occasional sips of tea from the mug, as I'd have liked. Although it was nice to be giving my wife a cuddle, the knowledge that my tea was getting colder and colder by the second (yet again!) meant I simply couldn't relax and enjoy the cuddle. My conversation became increasingly stilted, plus I kept glancing at the mug to check if steam was still rising from it. Mary picked up on this and got a bit cross and eventually pushed me away, meaning my hands were now free to have a sip of tea. But guess what? Yep, by then the tea was stone cold and required reheating. (Yet again!)

John's Explanatory Note: Each time you reheat the tea it will develop a bit more of a funny metallic flavour until eventually it tastes really horrible, and then – I'm afraid there's nothing for it but to chuck it and put the kettle back on.

I'm no mathematician but it's obvious that the number of times you have to reheat your tea is in direct proportion to how busy or distracted you are. Surprise surprise! I've written a song about that too. Before we hear it, we should consider one further dilemma that is the cause of much 'microwave misery', to the extent that one local microwave user (Mr Ken Worthington Esq.) has totally lost confidence in the product.

How do you guarantee that the microwave plate won't come off the plastic thingy in the middle?

The simple answer is: there IS no guarantee. Well, did you see that clause in the guarantee for your microwave after you bought it? Did it say:

> The manufacturer guarantees that the microwave plate will never at any time in any circumstances slip off the plastic thingy in the middle. If it does, the manufacturer guarantees that the user will be able to replace it easily and in less than 30 seconds, or your money back.

No, you didn't read that, because they know it can't be done, and they don't want to risk being sued by millions of disgruntled users!

I'm rather embarrassed that I can't remember the name of the plastic thingy that the plate sits on, and unbelievably I can't locate the manual just now. But a quick look on the internet has revealed that the 'thingy' is actually called the 'coupler' – it fits over the shaft in the centre of the microwave oven cavity floor, and must remain in situ at all times!

So now we know. I have also discovered that the inventor of the microwave oven is an American electrical engineer called Percy Spencer (1894–1970). That's interesting: Percy passed away just three years before Ken appeared on *New Faces*, but long before microwave oven prices tumbled sufficiently for most people (including the Shuttleworth family) to purchase them. Now they're only thirty quid, aren't they, and within the grasp of everyone. But

Me adjusting our gate's action. Note how the absence of a kneeling pad is forcing me to squat on my haunches, thereby exercising several key muscle groups including the quadriceps and the calves.

don't get too close to them, obviously, or you'll come down with radiation sickness!

Ken and microwaves

In my humble view, Ken Worthington should never be allowed near a microwave oven, and I'll tell you for why. Firstly, his microwave plate always comes off the 'coupler' (ooh, I do like that word, and I'm so glad that I now know it!), and has to be relocated, but Ken has no patience, so he always gives up and leaves the plate at a funny angle, meaning the sauce of the lasagne (or whatever 'meal for one' he's heating up) overflows onto the microwave plate, soiling it. Subsequent wiping of the plate to remove the sauce stains only dislodges the plate further, increasing Ken's despair. I've been called round to help Ken relocate the plate onto the coupler on several occasions in the past, but despite successfully doing so, it always goes wonky again a few hours later.

Once, Ken blew up his microwave oven by foolishly placing a metallic tray containing leftover curry directly into the microwave without transferring it first to a microwaveable dish. He turned up at our house with his cold curry in a burnt-out metal tray. It was a windy night, his Afro was blowing everywhere and he was looking decidedly sheepish. Mary and I had a brief private discussion, leaving Ken on the doorstep, before agreeing to admit Ken and allow him to reheat his leftovers in our microwave oven. But he was monitored at all times – the transferring of his curry from a metal dish to a microwaveable container was overseen by Mary, and as soon as Ken had quit the premises I gave the microwave a thorough cleaning out with a micro-cloth and powerful anti-bacterial spray (scented).

In conclusion, some readers may consider that Ken should be banned from ever owning a microwave again, and while I'd wholeheartedly agree with you, I fear it would be extremely hard to legally enforce.

Right, let's have a singsong!

BUSY DAY

From the very moment I woke to Wogan
I've had a load on
'Don't stop till you drop' has been my slogan
I'm not complaining, all I'm saying
Is that from 8 a.m.
It's been absolute mayhem

Work, work all day long
Constantly in a flap
I make the busiest bee look about
As busy as Andy Capp!

It's been a very busy day
Honestly I've not stopped
Rushing around, I've not sat down
And now I'm ready to drop
It's been a very busy day
I've barely had time to shave
I've lost count of the number of times
I've reheated my tea in the microwave

They say a woman's work is never done.
Well, I'll tell you, chum,
This man's work has barely begun
And yet if you should ask, I can't recall
A single job at all
You don't when your back's against the wall

Work, work all day long
No time for a nap
Just a quick 'campacinno'
And a tuna mayo bap

It's been a very busy day
Honestly I've not stopped
Rushing around, I've not sat down
And now I'm ready to drop
It's been a very busy day
I've barely had time to shave
I've lost count of the number of times
I've reheated my tea in the microwave

I've just had a worrying thought – if Ken comes home after a bad day and happens to glance down at his welcome mat, seeing the message 'Goodbye World' might tempt him to end it all, perhaps by drinking a whole bottle of Malibu in one go? (That's Ken's favourite tipple, by the way.) Ken is prone to self-harming, I'm sorry to say. Here's an example: I once watched him clonk his head repeatedly with a big book after he'd added up my petrol expenses wrongly for a professional engagement which required me to dress as a Jacobean foot soldier while distributing leaflets advertising a car valeting service in Worksop. I'd pointed out Ken's error and clearly he wasn't happy! On that occasion, Ken wasn't badly hurt as his thick Afro absorbed most of the impact but next time he might not be so lucky...

"Oh, hello, Mary! Have you drunk yer tea, love?" I say to Mary, who's just entered the lounge in her dressing gown.

"Yes," Mary replies. "I thought you were getting dressed, John, not lounging around on the settee."

"I will presently, love," I reply, calmly, refusing to be riled by Mary's insinuation. "I was going to feed Kirsty first."

"I've done it," Mary replies, quickly. "She's been in the garden and is back in her basket."

"Oh good," I reply, gratefully. "Are we going to do a big shop later, love?"

"We don't need to," says Mary. "We went to Morrisons the other day, remember? We don't need anything."

"Oof, I'm sure we do, Mary," I suggest anxiously.

"No, we don't, John," Mary insists, sharply, "but you need to go and jump in the shower – right now, please!"

"I will shortly, love!" I say, adding hopefully, "But first, Mary, I think you should check the cupboards to see if we're running low on any particular items, because you never know... I had quite a few custard-cream biscuits last night, and the packet will be almost empty."

"Well, that serves you right for being a greedy-guts," Mary retorts.

"Erm..." I continue, thinking hard – oof, this shopping trip is proving to be a hard sell – "Do we need any fromage frais, or a tin of spaghetti hoops perhaps? What about a jar of that pestio for when our Karen comes home?"

———————————

John's Explanatory Note: 'Pestio', as I believe it's called, is a substance like mould in a jar, which my daughter who's gone veggie likes to eat although I don't know why, but if it persuades Mary to embark on a supermarket shop I'll be delighted to purchase a jar. Just think of the shopping dilemmas we'll encounter, readers!

———————————

"Hmm," says Mary, clearly wavering. "Well, it's shepherd's pie for tea so I could use more stock cubes, and I can pick up my coat from the dry cleaner's afterwards, so go on then!"

"Fantastic, Mary," I reply, excitedly. "Just think of the dilemmas we'll encounter!"

"I'm sorry?" replies Mary, looking slightly baffled.

"Oof, well, erm…"

I didn't mean to spill the beans so early on, as I know Mary might clam up if I tell her I'm writing a book. Her contributions may become stilted and self-conscious, and I want her to speak from the heart. Still, she's going to find out sooner or later, so there's nothing for it but to tell her…

"Erm, I'm writing a book today, love – all about domestic dilemmas, and your contributions would I'm sure be eagerly devoured by the readers."

"I beg your pardon?" says Mary, this time looking baffled AND slightly worried.

"Well, you know, the readers would like it if you could give us your view on certain dilemmas, and as we're in the lounge and I've just opened the curtains, why don't we start with 'curtain opening' dilemmas?"

"Readers? Curtains? What's going on, John? Have you borrowed Ken's video camera again? I'm still in my dressing gown, you know!" says Mary, hurrying from the lounge to dash back upstairs.

———————

John's Explanatory Note: You might be wondering why Mary didn't spot me writing my book, so I suppose it's about time I revealed that although I am scribbling some thoughts down – as and when they come to me – much of this book is being recorded on a dictaphone (hidden in my jacket pocket). It just makes things easier, you see, readers, and allows me to capture everything that happens today, especially all those dilemmas!

———————

Oof, I should have approached Mary a bit more carefully. I don't want to put her off – as an experienced mother of two AND a professional dinner lady, Mary's contributions to a book on domestic dilemmas will be highly valued. But they're going to be hard to obtain, I can tell that already.

Hm… What shall I do now? Ideally, I'd like to chill for a bit and watch *Homes under the Hammer* with the effervescent Martin Roberts, that lad with the big tummy, which he tries to hide under his stylish leather coat. But I don't want to anger Mary further, so I'll go and jump in the shower, as requested. Besides, the bathroom environment presents dozens of important dilemmas – fantastic! But before I do that I'll just readjust the lounge curtains.

Ooh, I notice there's a hem dangerously close to Mary's shepherdess on the window sill. If Mary had got involved then she'd surely have noticed that, and had a go at me, so it's just as well she didn't! I'll ask her to contribute a bit later, when we're out shopping and she's forgotten all about me writing a book. See you in the next chapter… I'm going to go and jump in the shower now!

CHAPTER 3:

BAD BATHROOM BEHAVIOUR
(AND HOW TO AVOID IT)

Oof, I've just agreed to jump in the shower. Why did I do that? I might as well have signed my own death warrant! When people tell you to go and jump in the shower, there's only one thing you should do – ignore them! If you jump in the shower what's going to happen? You're going to slip and crack your head on the porcelain tiles, that's what. And then you'll be going to hospital, without having had a shower first!

Rule one

Always climb into the shower in a gingerly fashion and if necessary steady yourself as you do so. Not by gripping the shower curtain, as you're likely to pull it off its hooks if you lose your balance and it takes ages to reattach them. (Although this can be a very satisfying activity, as I know because I often reattach our shower curtain after Mary has washed it – on a very high-temperature wash to kill any lurking bacteria.)

Erm, I've just realised there is only one rule. There will be no *Rule two*, sorry about that.

Safe entry method for domestic shower users

As I say, steady yourself as you make your entry. Spread out your palms until they present the largest possible surface area and place them flat against the tiles before entering the shower. If you wet your hands first it may create a bit of suction on the tiles for extra safety. I've never tried that, but I just thought of it, so if anyone tries it and wants to give me some feedback about it, please don't hesitate to get in contact. (Obviously, I'm not prepared to give out my address to strangers, so I'm not sure how I'll receive your feedback, but still...)

Once you're safely in the shower you can do a little dance or wiggle your hips if you want to, but keep foot movement to a minimum, and remember: at all points during your shower experience there must be NO JUMPING!

Rainforest showers

Some posh people don't have a raised shower tray any more or a nice flowery curtain. Some don't even have a shower cubicle with a door. Instead, you just wander into the shower, like it's the start of a maze. Sometimes it even involves going round a corner before you come to the shower. What's all that about then! It's highly confusing. And the water isn't dispensed from a removable plastic shower head on the wall. It comes from something that resembles an upturned steel colander and the water cascades down on top of you like you're in the Amazon rainforest! That might be some people's idea of heaven, but I'm not convinced. Won't the water pummel your head from on high and eventually crush it?

Ken Worthington has one of those posh showers and just shrugs when I express any concerns, but that could be because he sports an Afro, which will absorb the impact of the water. Well, if you want to have water drumming down on your head – on your own head be it, if you know what I mean!

Soap or shower gel?

You may think there's no dilemma here – it's shower gel every time, surely? Well, you may be right, or you may be wrong. Let's put a historical perspective on this: thirty-five years ago we had no hesitation in reaching for the soap. I believe shower gel had become publicly available by then but did anyone use it? Not on your nelly... or your belly either! Oof, that was meant to be a joke but I'm not sure it was that funny!

Back then soap was king, and to illustrate my point, remember how excited the world was when Shield soap emerged in the mid-seventies? No, you don't? Where were you then? Clearly, not in the bath! I recall rubbing Shield soap up and down my leg in the bath and being awestruck by its eerie shade of blue, not to mention the exotic streaks or 'marbling effect' that ran through the whole bar. It was as if the soap had come from outer space, but ooh, I hope it blinking well didn't because then it would be radioactive and harmful to humans. Hmm, I might write to the manufacturers and check that it isn't...

When shower gel came into our lives in the early eighties we'd not seen anything like it before and the public were confused. Not a dissimilar situation to when Curly Wurlys were introduced and we didn't recognise the packaging, so everyone thought a Curly Wurly was a packet of sparklers, and we were understandably wary about putting them in our mouths – do you remember? Possibly not, so let me remind you...

How I met Ken Worthington

It was the late seventies and Ken had just moved in next door to us. He was standing in his garden underneath his carport. I approached him intending to say hello and welcome him to the neighbourhood.

John's Explanatory Note: I also intended to ask Ken what route he'd taken to get here, enquire about traffic conditions en route, his opinion of the removal men, etc. Did he need to borrow any sugar? (Hopefully not as I recall we were running quite low ourselves at the time!)

But before I could ask him anything I was stopped dead in my tracks by the sight of Ken eating a packet of sparklers. Yes, you heard me right – A PACKET OF SPARKLERS!

"What a strange man!" I thought, and naturally I kept my distance. He still hadn't noticed me so I bobbed down behind the hedge and rested on my haunches for a while, so I could observe him undetected through the gap between two miniature conifers that run along the border between our two properties.

After a while I saw the words 'Curly Wurly' on the sparklers packet from which he appeared to be eating, and realised that no self-respecting sparkler manufacturer would call their product by such a silly name. I watched as the strange man munched away, and bits of toffee appeared to be catching on his teeth. He was making appreciative noises and producing a fair amount of saliva. It

COULDN'T be a packet of sparklers – it HAD to be a chocolate bar! I bobbed up again and formally introduced myself to Ken, who immediately offered me a bite of the Curly Wurly, but as I still wasn't 100 per cent sure what it was, and because I didn't know Ken very well at that stage, I declined his offer. I wish I hadn't now because the Curly Wurly is one of my favourite items of confectionery.

John's Explanatory Note: Curly Wurlys are made a bit smaller now than they used to be, as you may or may not have noticed. Ironically, so too are packets of sparklers, so the comparison still exists – it's a crazy old world, isn't it, readers!

Why does shower gel resemble Swarfega?

Back to shower gel… as I've already stated, we'd not seen a product like it before. Well, we had – it's called Swarfega! So initially everyone thought shower gel must really be Swarfega and avoided it like the plague. Then at some point, someone – I don't know who, but a very brave person indeed – took their life in their hands and got in the shower with a bottle of shower gel and discovered that in fact it was lovely. It really did get you clean, and without stripping off a layer of your skin. Word soon got round and soap was swiftly abandoned, though not without some resistance by diehard soap users like Alan the Opera Singer (a local entertainer also on the books of agent Ken Worthington), who confided in me on a day trip to Riber Castle in 2016 that he prefers soap.

In conclusion, hats off to the inventor of shower gel – a great product, well done, but why on earth did you have to make it resemble Swarfega? You slipped up badly there, my friend!

Now, years later, after we've all got used to shower gel and the bar of soap is sitting neglected in the soap tray, something has happened to shower gel to make me question whether we should still be using it. What's happened? Surely you've noticed? It's gone all gloopy and viscous, so once applied it just slips off your body in a big lump and lands in the shower tray. Or it's the opposite problem: it's too thin, so it just runs off you before you can lather up. Either way it slips into the blinking shower tray and your instinct then is to try and scoop it up with your foot and disperse it over your leg, but don't do that!

Why not? Because you'll be on one leg, won't you, and likely to topple over and then you'll grab hold of the shower curtain and pull it down off the rail, ripping the curtain and damaging the hooks, etc., AND you'll crack your head on the shower tray. You might as well have jumped in the shower! Why, oh why – just when the public were getting confident with the product – did they decide to mess with the consistency of shower gel and force us all to go back to soap?

But what soap? I can't see any!

Neither can I. It's gone. There are no bars anywhere in the house any more, and it's a blinking disgrace! Oh yes, there's a bit of dried-up green soap somewhere – possibly in the garage – or it might be a multi-coloured misshapen mess of several old bars crushed together, but the only readily accessible soap in the house is:

Liquid soap (will the bubbles burst?)

While years of competition with shower gel have slowly killed off the bar of soap, there's a new kid on the block that has further eroded conventional soap sales. Its sudden popularity has ruffled some feathers in the Shuttleworth household, I have to say, and I know Alan the Opera Singer isn't too happy that his wife Pauline has a bottle of liquid soap in every sink in the house. Sometimes it doesn't sit in the shape of the sink lip very well, and the bottle has been known to topple over. Alan just shakes his head and says nothing when I mention that fact, but that doesn't mean he doesn't care about the issue deeply. I know he's hopping mad about it!

Right, I'm going to sing all about liquid soap now, if you don't mind. (I was going to discuss the importance of knowing whether your face flannel is being used by other family members for cleaning the bath, but I'm too angry about the soap situation, so we'll leave it, if you don't mind.)

BARS OF SOAP (ARE DISAPPEARING)

I get in a lather
When I see that there's no bar there
No bar of soap by the kitchen sink
The soap's now in a bottle
Its inventor I could throttle
For soon the bar of soap will be extinct

Bars of soap are disappearing
Soap dispensers are all the rage
Bars of soap are disappearing
And not because of everyday usage

I get in a lather
When I see that there's no bar there
No bar of soap by the kitchen sink
And there's none in the bathroom
Why not? There is enough room
Its absence in our house has caused a stink!

Soap dispensers are a distraction
Their appeal I don't understand
Though I admire the smooth pump action
As I dispense the soap into my hand

(*Feel free to punch the air as you reprise the chorus, readers. Here it comes...*)

Bars of soap are disappearing
Soap dispensers are all the rage
Bars of soap are disappearing
And not because of everyday usage

(*Bring back the soap!!*)

Should you sing in the shower?

Oof, I've still not had my shower, readers. I was going to sing that last number while I showered but instead I performed it in front of the mirror while clutching Mary's bar of Camay. I was squeezing it hard (as I was quite cross), and it's now badly misshapen. Mary won't be happy if she clocks it looking like this. I'd better get in the shower (climbing gingerly, NOT jumping, remember) and rub myself with soap, in the hope that my finger impressions will be smoothed out of existence.

And as I shower, I shall sing another song, which brings me on to the delicate subject of singing in the bathroom, either in the shower or in the bath, or even on the bathroom scales (not advisable as any attempt at vibrato will make the needle on the scales wobble, providing an inaccurate reading).

I mentioned vibrato just then and it's something I can do rather well, if I say so myself. After all, I'm a versatile singer/organist of many years' experience, as my sole agent Ken Worthington will testify. Now, I'm not being rude but I suspect most readers won't have a terribly good command of vibrato. I'm right, aren't I? Please don't beat yourself up about it. It's quite normal to not be very good at singing. If that's you, then your dilemma is this: should you be inflicting your singing voice on the rest of house? Wouldn't it be better to keep quiet as you concentrate on your ablutions? Spraying on deodorant requires a lot of concentration − locating the nozzle so that you direct the spray correctly, unblocking the nozzle if it's become blocked (with the bristles of your toothbrush? Ooh no − that's dirty!) − and so is best done in silence.

––––––––

John's Explanatory Note: An old toothbrush could be used for such a task, but it should be kept on its own shelf in the bathroom cabinet. Incidentally, toothbrush and toothpaste dilemmas are too numerous and complex to discuss here. They are discussed in depth in their own chapter near the end of this book, thank you!

––––––––

As I was saying... shaving too needs to be undertaken in absolute silence, as any sudden jaw movements could be highly dangerous. Look, what I'm trying to say is: sing if you really have to, but maybe just hum softly to yourself? That'd be safer for everybody, wouldn't it? I'm sorry I'm being a bit negative about your singing. Maybe it's because I'm getting low on energy as I'm hungry and need my breakfast. I'm sure you've got a lovely voice, although please remember you might be fooling yourself as the echo off the bathroom tiles tends to make it sound more lovely than it really is!

Oof... there! I'm in the shower now and am going to end this chapter by singing a song which explains the importance of singing with vibrato. You'll notice the second verse refers to tap dancing and a clarinettist. That's because it was originally sung by Ken Worthington. But if you don't mind I'm not inviting him into the shower to sing it with me!

A GOOD COMMAND OF VIBRATO

When I was a little boy, my father said to me
"You sound just like a strangled cat, a singer you'll never be"
So what if my dulcet tones have never been admired?
A good command of vibrato is all that is required

I'd like to pose a question, but I'll begin with an answer
A clarinettist I am first, and second a tap dancer
But why should I not sing as well if I feel so inspired?
A good command of vibrato is all that is required

A good command of vibrato is all that is required
No need to wear a snazzy suit, or be lavishly attired
Don't worry if no karaoke unit has been hired
A good command of vibrato is all that is required

*(Everybody – even if you're rubbish at singing and you've
absolutely no command of vibrato!)*
Yes, a good command of vibrato is all that is required
A good command of vibrato is ALL THAT IS REQUIRED!

CHAPTER 4:

SERIAL CEREAL EATER

I'm down in the kitchen now all showered and dressed in freshly laundered clothing, and I'm ready to eat my breakfast. Some of you will be wondering why I didn't have my breakfast while I was still in my pyjamas and dressing gown, but if I had considered doing that (and believe you me – I did!), it would have meant discussing another dilemma that would have taken up twenty pages at least!

All right then – let's spend half a page discussing that dilemma, as it IS important, I do realise, and it's crazy to think we can avoid discussing the matter.

Should you have breakfast before or after you get dressed?

On a Sunday I have been known to make toast in my dressing gown, but on a weekday I fervently believe you should be washed and dressed before you sit down to your breakfast. If you don't, and every morning you walk around bleary-eyed in your pyjamas or nightie while munching a bowl of cereal, well, it's dirty and slovenly, isn't it, and faced with the knowledge that you should be dressed, feelings of self-loathing will envelop you (unless you're a teenager – they seem immune to this problem), and could lead to depression and possibly mental illness, and even result in your going back to bed.

―――――――

John's Explanatory Note: After food intake the body often craves a nice lie-down to aid digestion. If you're already dressed in your nightclothes, and feeling a bit down to boot, returning to your bed may prove irresistible!

―――――――

There's another problem associated with consuming cereal while you're not yet fully awake – it could be risky in terms of grain and milk spillages on your dressing gown. Coordination between hand and mouth will be poor, as will your sense of when your bowl is horizontal, so is it really worth the risk?

Cubans on the wall

Ken Worthington clearly thinks it IS worth the risk as he often has breakfast in his jimjams, in summer months outside on his patio with his bowl placed securely on the table (I presume it's horizontal, although I've not had my spirit level on it to check). Ken also has those posh croissants and a mini pot of raspberry conserve, the seal of which I've observed him expertly break on many an occasion, usually when I've been in the garden with my Workmate sanding down a strip of beading prior to securing it with panel pins, plus wood glue, if deemed necessary.

My worried expression suggests I've just spotted Ken eating a bowl of cereal on the low boundary wall, but it's probably just because I'm wanting the photographer (Alan the Opera Singer, as I recall) to hurry up so I can get on with my DIY!

On a more sinister note: those mini pots of conserve are what you tend to find in bed and breakfasts and hotels, which begs the question: is Ken stealing them from various establishments when he stays there on business, and smuggling them out in his bumbag? I think he might be, and whether or not I should report him to the police for this felony provokes another dilemma – do I shop a friend or remain an accessory to a crime? It's not a domestic dilemma though, is it, really… so I think best to leave it for now.

As I've already stated, Ken has been spotted walking along the low boundary wall that separates his garden from mine, humming to himself and even doing a spoof tap-dance routine while clutching a bowl of cereal. It's behaviour that beggars belief, and if I hadn't seen it with my own eyes I wouldn't have thought it possible that a grown man could act in such a way. What makes it even more unbelievable is that, although he's fully dressed by this time, Ken's footwear is totally unsuitable – Cuban heel boots! Dancing in Cuban heels on a brick wall while eating cereal is highly perilous, readers. It's a crazy thing to do, so please don't ever do it!

What if the dishwasher door is open, making pedestrian access around the kitchen extremely difficult?

I knew this dilemma was going to be raised and don't worry, I'm fully prepared to tackle it. It doesn't mean I have the solution though. I warn you now – it's a tricky one!

The obvious solution is to shut the dishwasher door and get on with making your breakfast, but that could be dangerous for the following reason: your partner (or flatmate) might get angry that you've shut the dishwasher without first loading or unloading it, depending on the reason that they've left it open. Either way, it's been left open as a clear hint that you have a job to do!

So from this we can see that it would be extremely foolhardy to close the dishwasher door and proceed with a leisurely breakfast, as your wife or husband (or even the 'non-binary numbers' for these enlightened times) will no doubt enter the kitchen at some point and notice what you've done, and give you an earful, which could put you right off your Frosties if that's what you're having. (Choice-of-cereal dilemma coming soon!)

So, the dilemma is: do you have the heart to empty or refill the dishwasher before you have your breakfast, or do you have the stomach to sustain a verbal attack from your partner for not doing so? I told you it's a tricky one! All I'll say is this: how will you cope with putting away or placing in the dishwasher all those heavy pans on an empty stomach? The answer is: you won't. So, I reckon you should have your breakfast first and risk an ear-bashing. However, you then you risk an ankle-bashing!

How can you avoid bashing your ankles on and even tripping over the open dishwasher door?

It's very difficult, nay, impossible to avoid catching your ankles on the open dishwasher door and I reckon this is why world leaders don't even discuss the problem. How can they when it's insurmountable? There really is no way round it, readers – you're going to bash your ankles on it at some point, usually after you've got your cereal bowl and you turn back to get a spoon from the drawer, OR you're dashing to the toaster because you can smell burning toast, so, my advice is – just accept it.

John's Explanatory Note: This is another reason why you should get dressed before you have your breakfast – you can don thick socks and high-ankled boots to minimise any bruising received when your shins collide with the door. I'm sorry I can't offer any proper solutions to this one but there really aren't any, so let's just move swiftly on to the next section.

Cereal Selection — how do I know which is the right one for me?

Well now, this could be a dilemma, as there are dozens of different cereals commercially available. In the old days choosing was easy — you bought the packet that came with a free toy. Sadly, nowadays that option doesn't seem to be available, so my advice is — if you don't want to have a 'cereal choosing' dilemma — be like me and choose every single cereal available! Song time! Punch the air and join me in becoming a...

SERIAL CEREAL EATER

When I wake up in the morning
I get washed and dressed
My hair is combed and neatly parted
I like to look my best
A clean white hanky is selected
From the middle drawer
Then I make my way into the kitchen
Can you guess what for?

To eat my breakfast, yes,
But not fried eggs and bacon
If you think I'm a cooked-breakfast man
You're very much mistaken
Not even toast and marmalade
For that, I have no room
The reason for this will become
Apparent very soon

I'm a serial cereal eater
A serial cereal eater
How does it feel to meet a
Serial cereal eater?
Cornflakes, Frosties, Sugar Puffs
And that new one, Optivita
I just cannot get enough
I'm a serial cereal eater

You may be amazed by the amount of maize
I munch each morn
Yes, so am I, and what about the corn?
The corn I carry on consuming
Deep into the day
Weetabix for elevenses
For afternoon tea – Special K

I'm a serial cereal eater
A serial cereal eater
How does it feel to meet a
Serial cereal eater?
Cornflakes, Frosties, Sugar Puffs
And that new one, Optivita
I just cannot get enough
I'm a serial cereal eater

I guess it's a pretty fair assumption
If I don't want to die
I'll have to cut down my consumption
But how, how can I?

*(Ooh, I could murder a bowl of Coco Pops. Hey – murder... maybe I'm
a serial cereal killer? No, that was just a joke, and a very poor one...)*

SERIAL CEREAL EATER

I'm a serial cereal eater
A serial cereal eater
How does it feel to meet a
Serial cereal eater?
Cornflakes, Frosties, Sugar Puffs
And that new one, Optivita
I just cannot get enough
I'm a serial cereal eater
I'm a SERIAL CEREAL EATER!

I was lying when I said I liked every cereal. I don't like Optivita and only mentioned it in the song because it rhymes with 'eater'. Sorry if you're feeling duped, but listen, has anyone even tried Optivita? Possibly, but I've yet to meet them. It's too posh and too pricey, and that's probably why it was eventually removed from the supermarket shelves, every single packet unsold, I assume. Unfortunately, it was replaced with another one that's a bit dear, an' all: Curiously Cinnamon. Oof, just the name sends shivers down yer spine. To me it suggests a consignment of drugs from the Orient, do you know what I mean? Shame, as I believe it used to be called Cinnamon Grahams. I liked the cereal then, as the name conjured up an elderly gentleman munching on a nutritious biscuit!

CHAPTER 5:

CRUMBS, THERE'S NO CRUMB TRAY!

Well, I've just had two bowlfuls of Wheatos plus a bowl of Sultana Bran (for extra fibre), so you may be surprised to learn I'm having a slice of toast to follow. I don't want to, as I've no room, but I need to in order to examine the dilemmas associated with making toast.

I'm just with our pop-up toaster now, checking the spring mechanism which enables the toast to pop up when the toasting cycle is complete. I'm examining the mains plug for damage and wear and tear, and checking that the crumb tray is empty, which, erm, it is, excellent! Incidentally, my wife Mary seems to think that a crumb tray is a basic feature of the pop-up toaster, but she's very wide of the mark in that supposition. It's a luxury add-on, readers, and anyone proposing to buy a new toaster, or – if you're watching the coppers this month – scouring the listings on eBay for a second-hand one, should bear that in mind.

———————

John's Explanatory Note: An adjustable bread-width gauge is also a luxury add-on, but a choice of browning settings should be provided as standard. And a plug fitted with a 13 amp fuse. And a box, and hopefully an instruction manual!

———————

"Who are you talking to?" asks Mary, as she enters the kitchen and switches on the kettle.

"Oh, hello Mary," I reply, casually – confident that Mary hasn't realised I'm still recording on my dictaphone. "I was just thinking aloud before offering up two slices of bread to our toaster."

"Are you indeed! Well, you'll need to turn the toaster the right way up then!" advises Mary before making herself an instant coffee and returning to the lounge to watch – I'm guessing, looking at the kitchen clock – *Wanted Down Under.*

———————

Interestingly enough, we won our current toaster on eBay, and I'm happy to announce it DOES boast a crumb tray. We love it to bits and use it daily, but the emotional journey we had to endure in order to get it makes me wonder, was it all really worth it? I don't like to talk about it, and I'm not sure Mary is in the right mood to discuss the matter. Hm… I KNOW! I'll sing you a song I wrote all about it.

THE TOASTER SONG

We're watching a toaster on eBay
Hoping that we may
Soon be the owners
The experience has been so wearing
Tempers are flaring
The ordeal has thrown us

But don't you worry, Mary
I know the waiting's scary
But keep your nerve and in no time
That toaster will be yours and mine

Should Mary increase our bid like I told her?
Well, circumstances may force her
If we are outbid
I'll be so glad when this auction is over
And we have a new toaster
For less than a quid

Don't you worry, Mary
I know the waiting's scary
I know that you are itching
To see that toaster in our kitchen

*I currently have a toaster, but it doesn't boast a crumb tray.
What should I do?*

What do you WANT to do? How desperate are you to own a
toaster with a crumb tray? Do you lie awake at night wishing you
had one, or are you not that bothered and so have an undisturbed
sleeping pattern? If the former – get out there and buy a toaster
with a crumb tray today, or tomorrow if it's getting bit late now.

If the latter, then accept that you're probably going to spend the rest of your life regularly lifting up your toaster (both hands please!), turning it upside down and gently shaking it so all the crumbs trapped inside the toaster come tumbling out onto the worktop. Prior to this, the toaster should have been unplugged, and all children and pets moved to another room and the door shut on them. Ooh, that seems a bit harsh, so maybe they can stay and watch – although obviously from a safe distance. Then with a clean dishcloth the crumbs should be gathered up and steered towards a receptacle held against the edge of the worktop, and transferred to a bin. Or if you'd rather, just scoop them into your hand and chuck 'em out for the birds.

I have a toaster that boasts a crumb tray, or plan to get one very shortly

Well, good for you – you must be feeling pretty smug, and with justification. However, with a crumb tray comes responsibilities, my friend. Well, just one really. You have to monitor it constantly and empty it when it's full. I'm in the kitchen now and I'm making myself some toast, as I've already stated. Once the toast has been buttered and the topping of my choice spread on to the toast, I will, erm… eat it. But then the crumb tray will be inspected, and if it's deemed to be at full capacity, it will have to be emptied.

What if I forget I've got a crumb tray, and fail to empty it?

Then you don't deserve to own a toaster with a crumb tray! I said that very thing to Ken Worthington, who once let his crumb tray get so full that the crumbs became badly charred and billowing smoke was produced during the toasting cycle. It set off his smoke alarm, which luckily I heard (I was in the garden rewinding a hosepipe that had a slight kink in it) and, fearing the worst, dashed to Ken's assistance. Once the smoke had cleared and the alarm had been reset I sat Ken down on his kitchen bar stool – his legs were still swinging as they don't quite reach the crossbar cos he's quite short, you know, but that's by the way – and I talked quietly and calmly to him while issuing the following advice, which I dearly hope you will heed also.

———————

John's Explanatory Note: I didn't bob down on my haunches like just before I first met Ken. I thought about it but I would've been too low down, and my head would've been thrust back at a funny angle while talking to Ken. You know, he's not that diddy! Anyway, this is what I said to Ken:

———————

Check your crumb tray daily, Ken. Just because you emptied it yesterday, you can't assume it's not full or close to overflowing today. Different types of bread create different quantities of crumbs. Always remove your slices of toast slowly from the toaster, once the toasting cycle is complete, taking care not to snag the toast on the sides of the toasting slot, because if you do even more crumbs will be shed from the freshly made toast, adding to the crumbs already in the crumb tray.

As I recall, Ken said, "Shut your cake hole! I'm not listening to any more of this, John. Just shut up!" Now, although you might think that was an incredibly rude and ungrateful thing to say, unbeknown to Ken I'd come to the end of my advice, so although he thought he'd shut me up, he hadn't at all! I was going to stop talking at that point anyway, and return to my hosepipe, which was of far more concern to me than telling a foolish neighbour facts he should have known in the first place!

Having said that, my advice seems to have hit home. I've not heard Ken's smoke alarm go off since. (Hmm, I hope he hasn't just removed the battery?) And now you have heard the same excellent advice on this particular domestic dilemma, I do trust you will immediately put it into practice. Good luck to you, whether you've a crumb tray or not. I'm going to finish singing my song now...

Ohh! I can see us now in our dressing gowns
Early on a Sunday
You at the table, munching toast
Me emptying the crumb tray

Don't you worry, Mary
I know the waiting's scary
But keep your nerve and come Monday
We'll be filling up that crumb tray
Oh ho ho!

Unfortunately, we were blinkin' well outbid – the toaster went for £2.15. Doh! Although we were gutted, it was a blessing in disguise, for the item, I later realised, was located in Buckinghamshire, and my petrol costs to collect the toaster would have been astronomical! As it happened, I went straight back on eBay and found a much better toaster, with a superior-looking crumb tray, plus it had two extra browning settings, and, incredibly, we won it unopposed for 99p! The icing on the cake was that the item was located in the charming Derbyshire village of Hathersage, a mere ten miles from Sheffield, so my petrol costs were minimal, and a pleasant day trip was planned around the item collection. This included a comfort break at a Total garage in Beauchief where Mary and I enjoyed the 'coffee and cake' deal operating at that time (sorry, I think it may have expired by now).

"Ooh, Mary – you made me jump!" I say to my wife who is standing in the kitchen doorway with her mug, just watching me. "Have you been there for some time? You shouldn't creep up on people like that!"

"Excuse me!" retorts Mary, testily, "I'm not creeping up on anybody. You're the one that's acting funny, talking to yourself all the time. I'm here to let you know that *Can't Pay? We'll Take it Away!* is about to start."

And with that, Mary turns on her heel and goes back into the lounge, leaving the pleasant aroma of instant coffee in her wake. I'm in a quandary, readers, and I knew this might happen. Do I follow Mary into the lounge and sit on the sofa with her and enjoy some nice late-morning television entertainment, or do I stay here and crack on with writing my book?

Oof, it's a domestic dilemma! But I've no choice, have I? No I haven't...

So, as I was saying, we collected the toaster from the seller in Hathersage and, erm... on the way back we didn't stop at that garage again to get another coffee and cake deal as, although tempted, we were a bit full and it was getting late. Upon our return home I checked my computer and discovered the vendor had already left us feedback. Without wishing to boast, it was very complimentary. 'Smooth transaction, hope to deal with again!' was the comment. Sadly though, all subsequent attempts to make contact with the vendor with a view to meeting up socially have met with failure. I WILL keep trying!

CHAPTER 6:

KEN'S KITCHEN KRISIS!

That's an eye-catching chapter title, I think you'll agree, even if 'crisis' is spelt wrong. I've just given my next-door neighbour and sole agent Ken Worthington a quick call and asked him to pop round to suggest some dilemmas for my book. Ken is well placed to advise – why, his whole life has been one huge dilemma! Oof, no, I don't mean that, that was a bit nasty. I'm very grateful to Ken because he's helped my career... erm... I was going to say 'enormously', but that's not true. 'Slightly', some might say, and some would argue he's held me back and I should have left his agency blinking years ago!

You see, I've been trying to make it as a versatile singer/organist for a long time now, and I'm still waiting for that big break. Yes, Ken negotiates petrol money for me when I play the hospice, but it's only a local hospice so the petrol money is just a few coppers, usually presented in a sealed brown envelope. Ooh, but I can't deny I do love the excitement of breaking the seal and counting the money inside. Having said that, it's a shame to rip the envelope when it could have been carefully steamed open and used again.

If the booking is further afield, Ken has been known to flex his negotiating muscles more impressively – he once got me 'unfettered access to the tea urn' and my own 'designated parking spot'. That was, I originally thought, a gig with Billy Joel, so I was very excited, as you can imagine. But Ken was gabbling indistinctly when he told me, and the 'gig with Billy Joel' turned out to be a 'gig in a village hall', which does sound very similar. Just try saying the two phrases out loud one after another: "A gig with Billy Joel… A gig in a village hall". They're practically identical, aren't they? Anyway, the gig (in a village hall) was cancelled in the end, but I only found out when I arrived. I'd just parked up in my designated spot when Ken rang my mobile to tell me the sad news, and because I wanted to park in it for a while at least, I just remained in my car and enjoyed the last of the oxtail soup in my flask (although, sadly, it had gone a bit cold).

Ah well, I must never lose sight of the fact that Ken once tasted the big time as 'TV's Clarinet Man', when he appeared on the TV talent show *New Faces* in 1973, so he is perfectly placed to offer me advice on all showbiz matters. Or is he? Oof, not really; as I've already stated, Ken came last on that particular edition and Tony Hatch crucified him.

Ken on New Faces *in 1973 – the true story*

While we wait for Ken to arrive to advise me on domestic dilemmas, let me tell you what REALLY happened on that fateful Saturday teatime in July 1973. I had the misfortune to catch that particular edition of *New Faces*, whereas some younger readers may have missed it. If so, were you out on your space hopper enjoying what remained of that sunny evening? Think back? Am I right? I suspect I might be. Some even younger readers would

A kitchen 'krisis' of my own is swiftly averted by a judicious application of interior Polyfilla. Although my mouth is closed, often during DIY tasks my mouth hangs open and my breathing becomes raspy — so claims my wife, Mary!

have missed seeing Ken because you weren't even born in 1973, were you!

John's Explanatory Note: Some of those who saw Ken on *New Faces* and would have read about it in this book, and corroborated my version of events, can't because they're now dead, and we're very sorry to hear that, but it can't be helped, I'm afraid.

Those who DID see Ken's performance had to endure him making a silly face to the camera, which ruined the atmosphere he'd painstakingly built up during the routine. It had begun well: Ken – sporting breeches, cavalier boots and cape (I don't think he had a sword, did he?) – was playing a jaunty tune on his clarinet as he spiralled round his wife at the time, Rhiannon, getting ever closer to her. She was wearing a long frilly frock and sat in a big wicker chair playing the harp. Then when Ken got to the epicentre he suddenly spun away as if to deny her. It was quite a clever routine really, well thought out with a fairy-tale ending, and going well until the camera came in for a close-up. Instead of doffing his cap (that's right, he had a baker's cap on like Hans Christian Andersen, you know, in the film when he sings 'The Ugly Duckling'), Ken went and made the silly face I've mentioned, like he'd seen a ghost, which led to Tony Hatch crucifying him.

Tony Hatch was renowned for giving contestants a right royal roasting if he didn't like their act, but never before had we seen Tony get so angry with a contestant for being rubbish. He was so angry with Ken that as I recall there was a bit of saliva at the side of his mouth, and I think a bubble appeared. It popped almost as soon as it had formed but... oof, I'm going to have to abandon the story now because the man himself has arrived. Yes, Ken Worthington has appeared at the kitchen window and is peering in trying to locate me, but the glare on the glass is making it difficult for him to see me. Is it my imagination, or is Ken making the same silly face he made on *New Faces* all those years ago?!

"Is that you, John?" Ken calls out.

I'm not replying. I remain crouched low beneath the breakfast bar.

"John? I've seen yer! I'm coming in."

Oof – luckily Ken won't be able to gain immediate access as our kitchen door, although not bolted, is on the catch preventing ne'er-do-wells or opportunist thieves from entering the property. Oof, he's trying the door and rattling it, which could alarm Mary while she sips her coffee in the lounge. Luckily, the TV's on loud and currently it sounds like someone is having a fight with a bailiff, so Mary won't hear the kerfuffle. Before I let Ken in, I'll just finish my story.

New Faces – *the fallout*

After Ken came last on *New Faces*, his wife Rhiannon left him and took up with a builder called Martin who lived in Stoney Middleton, and in desperation, Ken went to live in a caravan on the banks of a canal near the Dronfield bypass. And one night, he felt so low that he tried to take his life by jumping in the canal. But, you'll like this... Ken made the mistake of testing the temperature of the water first, and it was too cold for him, so cold that it brought Ken to his senses and he realised he just couldn't go through with it. Thank goodness, for Ken's sake, and mine too, and yours as well, readers. The only problem is this: since *New Faces*, Ken has become very shy and goes bright red when engaged in any kind of social interaction, as we're about to find out.

"Morning Ken! Do come in," I say to Ken, unlocking the kitchen door.

"Thanks, John!" Ken replies, going a bit red as he enters.

"Thank you for coming round, Ken," I say, courteously, "and at such short notice. But while it's lovely to see you, I hope you realise your visit must be fairly brief as I'll soon be going shopping with Mary."

"Oh, I see," says Ken, grunting a little as he climbs up onto our bar stool, which is a bit high for him. "Can I come too, John? I need to buy a bottle of Malibu and some edamame beans."

"Oof, Ken. Those are rather strange purchases, if you don't mind me saying. They certainly don't sit happily alongside the shopping list of a normal family like the Shuttleworths. It may confuse the readers. Erm, I don't know, Ken. You've put me on the spot there. While I'm flattered that you'd like to accompany us, I shall have to ask Mary first."

"Of course, John. I understand completely," replies Ken, graciously.

"Meanwhile, Ken," I continue, "why don't you get us in the mood for 'shopping dilemmas' by telling the readers about your recent shopping trip to Aldi, when you became distressed by the constant beeping noises at the till?"

"Listen, John," says Ken, his Afro bobbing up and down as he checks he's positioned centrally on the bar stool – at least, I presume that's what he's doing, "I'm delighted to hear you've finally started writing your book, and NOT BEFORE TIME, may I add?" Ken adds, settling on the stool, finally, "but can we just clear something up?"

"What's that, Ken?"

"Have you just been telling the readers about my appearance on *New Faces* in 1973?"

"No Ken, I haven't," I reply, dishonestly.

"I think you were," insists Ken, reddening further, his beady eyes peering out over his expensive tinted glasses. "I saw you through the window. You were mimicking that face I made, you know, like I'd just seen a ghost. You know I don't like you telling that story."

"You're mistaken, Ken." (Oof, how does he know? I thought he couldn't see me through the window!) "I was, erm... demonstrating the dilemma of deciding which carrier bags to choose before you commence your shopping trip, so as to avoid the 10p charge levied by all stores nowadays for carrier bags. You know, do you need to select bags which bear the logo of the store you're going to visit, or is it acceptable – is it even legal – to go in flaunting another store's bags? It's a dilemma that makes people anxious and sometimes just trying to decide what to do they pull a face like they've seen a ghost. That's what you must have seen through the window, Ken."

"Oh I see." (Phew! Ken's bought my story.) "Just remember, John, that as your sole agent I will be proofreading this book before it goes to the publishers, so anything that you've written before I arrived this morning will be clearly visible to me."

"I see." (Oof, I'd better tell the truth.) "Well, Ken, I WAS telling the readers about you making that face on *New Faces*. I apologise. But we can cut it out if you'd rather?"

"No, keep it in, John," replies Ken, tartly, as he leaps off the bar stool in one clean movement. "But I'm disappointed in you, and I'd appreciate it if you'd tell the truth immediately next time. Liars don't prosper!"

"No, they don't, Ken," I say, meekly, "and I'd love the opportunity to regain your trust. Tell me all about the trip to Aldi and I will write it down faithfully with no embellishments."

"I'm no longer in the mood, John. Good day to yer!" Ken shouts, walking to the door.

"Ken, please don't go just yet," I say, in a pleading tone. "You've not given me any of your domestic dilemmas."

"That's because I haven't got any!" replies Ken in a superior manner. "I'm very happy in my little bungalow and want for nothing, thank you!"

"But that's not true, Ken," I reply, knowingly. "What about all the problems you experience relocating the plate in your microwave once it's come off the coupler?"

"I manage fine!" splutters Ken, with a hint of bitterness.

"All right then," I continue, "what about the dilemma of losing the brush of your pink dustpan and brush set, so you are left with just the dustpan, which is pretty useless without the brush, let's face it. Do you chuck it away and buy a new dustpan and brush set, or do you hang on to that pink dustpan in the hope that the matching brush will one day turn up? It's a real-life dilemma that happened to YOU, Ken, because you told me all about it!"

"I don't remember that, John. When was that then?" says Ken, frowning, yet advancing back into the room, so my tactic is clearly working.

"Well, I do, Ken," I reply, getting a bit emotional and producing a lot of saliva suddenly – like Tony Hatch did – so that I have to wipe my mouth on my jumper, which is a bit slovenly, I realise, but no matter, it's important that Ken's story is told. "It was around 2013 or 2014, and you came round one morning very excited and told me that you'd found the brush again, and that 'there is no sweeter feeling than when you see a dustpan reunited with its brush.'"

"I would NEVER say THAT!" snorts Ken in disbelief. "That's what YOU said when YOU came round and noticed that I'd found the brush again… Don't you remember, yer nana?" Ken's looking at me angrily, his eyes blazing.

"Oh yes, Ken, you're right," I reply, suddenly remembering, and feeling a bit foolish. "Sorry, I forgot it was me who said that. And then I told you about my own experiences of dustpans and brushes becoming separated and how often you have to pair up mismatching items. And how it's humiliating to have a yellow brush that's slotted into a blue dustpan and you can detect the simmering anger of your wife each time she uses it. And although she's told you repeatedly that you need to buy a new dustpan and brush set – and publicly you agree with her – privately you're hanging on in the hope that somewhere in the house there's a yellow dustpan waiting to be reunited with its little brush."

"Hmm, I don't think you'll have any trouble filling your book with domestic dilemmas, John. Your head is clearly full of them!" sneers Ken, as he opens the kitchen door and walks out into the morning, his Cuban heels ringing noisily on our concrete flags, and receding as he… oof, now they're getting louder again. What's happening?

Ken's coming back into the kitchen. I wonder why? Ooh I say, now he's leaning in to my dictaphone.

"Good day to you, readers!" Ken says in a creepy tone, attempting a smile. "Catch up with you all later!"

Will he? That's rather presumptuous of him. I feel the moment is apt to sing a classic ballad I wrote after Ken refused to accept a birthday gift of a garden bench. The words fit this moment too.

POOR KEN AND THE BIRTHDAY BENCH

Ken's behaving like an ass
That's plain to see
But it must have been hard coming last
On *New Faces* in '73
Rhiannon, his wife, found another man
And bid Ken adieu,
And all she left were two wicker chairs
Which now attract mildew

Poor Ken, poor Ken
All alone in his big garden
Poor Ken, poor Ken
His spirit has been broken

Ken has told me he doesn't
Want another wife
But a garden bench will surely help
To rebuild his shattered life
For Rhiannon found another man
And bid Ken adieu
And all she left were two wicker chairs
Which now attract mildew

(*Everybody*) Poor Ken, poor Ken
His spirit has been broken
Poor Ken, poor Ken
But soon he will be laughing and joking *(let's hope so, anyway!)*

Now Ken's gone I can divulge what you've probably worked out already: he's a very highly strung man. Always has been. As a boy he used to wake up in a cold sweat and see a hooded axeman at the end of his bed. Ken told me that in confidence, but I felt you needed to be told. How awful, but it was Ken's fault really because he used to read scary comics like *Captain America* deep into the night. I used to read my *Tufty* magazine – I had a lovely night's sleep!

Ken's trip to Aldi (unembellished version)

Ken told me this story yesterday. Well, it's not really much of a story – he just said he was traumatised when he was in the queue at Aldi as it was very busy and all the tills were working flat out, and the combined beeping of all the items being scanned was just too much for Ken. He said it was suddenly crystal clear to him that the frantic beeping of the tills was like the squawking of electronic baby birds demanding to be fed, and that the store was like a huge electronic chicken coop. Ken said realising this made him feel very lonely and alienated from society, and he desperately craved eye contact and even conversation with the till assistant.

I said, "Ken, that was a crazy thing to try and do in a place like that – talk to someone? You should have had your head down concentrating on bagging your scanned items as quickly as possible so you weren't holding up the till assistant and the others in the queue, and then after a very quick 'bye' or 'cheers, buddy!' (which is a quite popular thing to say now, I believe), got the hell out of the store and back to your vehicle."

Ken fell silent and nodding slowly, considered my advice. I think he realised he was in the wrong and that by talking about electronic baby birds he had made himself appear foolish. Not as much as he did on *New Faces* in 1973 though, obviously!

CHAPTER 7:

HEY, HAVE YOU SEEN MY WIFE? (DISHWASHER DILEMMAS)

I'm sorry we've not gone shopping yet, readers. I'm still waiting for Mary, who has now popped upstairs.

"Mary!" I shout up the stairs. "When are we going shopping, love?"

"I'll be down shortly, John!" Mary calls, faintly. "While you're waiting, why don't you empty the dishwasher and then hoover the lounge?"

"Ooh... Good idea, Mary!"

It IS a good idea. Normally I wouldn't think so, but Mary has just raised an important domestic dilemma: when instructed to do the vacuuming, should you do it immediately and garner praise from your partner, thereby increasing the chance of receiving an extra turkey nugget on your plate next mealtime without even asking for it? Or do you ignore them and carry on reading the Subway leaflet that's just popped through the door, which features fabulous combi offers to be enjoyed that very month? You may regret it either way, but my advice is… erm… oof, it's a tricky one, because that Hearty Italian 12-incher looks most inviting. Erm… no, you do the hoovering! AND don't forget to put it away afterwards!

John's Explanatory Note: In the old days husbands only had to get the appliances out (vacuum cleaner, ironing board, washing basket, etc.), and then put them away again after their wives had used them. But since that #metoyou campaign, everything has changed. You have to do the bits in between, as well. And it's a good thing that we do have to. It's progress, lads!

I don't like to boast but I became a new man a long while back. Listen as I sing my song 'Modern Man', written way back in the mid-eighties!

MODERN MAN

I'm a modern man
I'm a modern man
I do the household chores
Whenever I can

I'm a modern man
I'm a modern man
I get the Hoover out
Then I put it away again… after my wife's finished using it, you
    know…

(Oof, sorry, I wasn't properly reconstructed back then, clearly!)

Then on Saturday morning I take an hour
Or two out of my life
To go shopping with Mary, my wife

(Yes indeed, and we WILL be going shopping — once I've finished singing this song!)

I'm a modern man
I'm a modern man
I do the washing up
Apart from the frying pan

(Cos you're best to leave that to soak, aren't you...?)

Hmm, nowadays Mary would just stick the frying pan in the dishwasher, but I'm old school. We've got a dishwasher, yes, but I don't trust it to clean items thoroughly. Emptying a dishwasher can take you hours as each washed item has to be examined closely, and if deemed unclean, placed back in the dishwasher. It begs the question (and presents the dilemma): "Should you even buy a dishwasher?"

Dishwasher dilemmas (Part 2)

We've already discussed the problem of bashing your ankles on the open dishwasher door. That should be enough to dissuade any sane person from buying a dishwasher, and for years the Shuttleworth family resisted. Mary wanted one badly because her friend Doreen Melody had one. (Doreen also has a camper van with a sturdy chrome ladder giving direct access to the roof — more of that later, I'm sure.) But I said, "No, Mary, we can't afford it." I wanted to wait until prices had tumbled sufficiently.

Just as we'd done when we wanted to buy a microwave oven in the eighties, in the early nineties I used to pay regular visits to Rumbelows to check if the price of dishwashers had come down enough, but they never did, so you could argue they were all wasted trips. But no, I enjoyed them thoroughly – checking out audio cassette recorders and pressing the Dolby button on and off, and then on and off again one more time (well, it made such a lovely satisfying click!); lifting electric cordless kettles off their bases and then replacing them. Ooh, you can't overestimate just how exciting that was to the general public when cordless kettles first came on the market, and I used to see a lot of Rumbelows' customers doing that – or if they weren't you could tell that they wanted to. There was also a nice grey swivel chair I used to sit on. (I'd only swivel slightly – I wouldn't bother trying to spin round lots of times like little kids do, tempting as it might be.)

I've just reminded myself of the fabulous kettle we used to own. It emitted an eerie blue light during the boiling cycle, which initially I was wary of as it struck me as something that would appeal to hallucinogenic drug users. Still, fascinated, I used to switch off the fluorescent strip light in our kitchen, sit on the bar stool and slip into a reverie as I watched the patterns the blue light made on the walls and ceiling as it shone through the rapidly bubbling water. The patterns reminded me of when I visited a discotheque one evening in the late seventies with some work colleagues from Comet.

———

John's Explanatory Note: Comet is where I worked, you see, and the store I finally bought our first microwave oven from, several years after I'd stopped working for the now defunct and sadly missed electrical chain. I know we're not supposed to be discussing microwaves, we should be discussing dishwashers, and

69

we will, but first let me just finish my story about the kettle (which we shouldn't really be discussing either!).

Well, we're actually on to discussing the disco now but we'll come back to the kettle shortly. I bought myself a lager shandy at the discotheque, and stood watching these lasses dancing in mm, quite short dresses for a while – they were jiggling around in a crazy blue light just like the kettle makes. It was almost psychedelic, which is drug inspired, isn't it? So I was a bit wary about it, and it's a good job I couldn't hang about. No, I had to leave early, as I had a table tennis match to attend. I used to play for the Sheffield YMCA F team, you see. That night we were playing against a team from a wire company in the Tinsley area, and they were very, very good, and we were roundly beaten.

The best way to explain how this blue-light kettle briefly changed our lives (sadly, it blew up one day and proved to be beyond economic repair) is to sing you a sad ballad all about it.

(I MISS MY) BLUE-LIGHT KETTLE

When we purchased it at Curry's
We were filled with doubts and worries
Could a blue-light kettle really fit the bill?
Was it worth the extra money?
Would it make the water taste funny?
But we absolutely loved it, and always will

I miss my blue-light kettle
Our current one's made of metal
But this one was made of plastic and was white
It made patterns on the ceiling
Which induced a pleasant feeling
When the boiling cycle was at its height

When we got it home and unwrapped it
Like children we reacted
Marvelling at the product we'd been sold
When it bróke we couldn't accept it
We wish we could have kept it
But all future cups of tea would have been cold!

I miss my blue-light kettle
Our current one's made of metal
But this one was made of plastic and was white
It made patterns on the ceiling
Which induced a pleasant feeling
When the boiling cycle was at its height
When the boiling cycle was at its height – agh agh agh!

(*The vocal goes a bit funny there, at the end, sorry about that…*)

Dishwasher dilemmas (Part 2, resumed, or is it Part 3 now?)

In the end, I think it was in February 2007, dishwasher prices tumbled enough for us to take the plunge and we bought a nice family-sized model from Argos. Our dishwasher is fully integrated, which means it fits snugly under the worktop and it's hidden behind a cupboard door so you can forget it's there. "What's the point in having a dishwasher if you forget it's there?" you may argue, and I wouldn't argue back – I'd agree with you. But you have to move with the times, I suppose.

But ooh, I do miss washing up by hand – the excitement of squirting washing-up liquid into a bowl of hot water and then agitating it rapidly with your hand to produce lots of bubbles. If in a fanciful mood, bubbles that were clinging to your rubber gloves could be raised to eye level and studied at leisure, and at this point you'd see one or two bubbles pop, which was disappointing, I suppose, but it wasn't really as there would still be so many that hadn't yet popped. Then you could blow vigorously and the bubbles sitting on your hand would float away – although actually most would fall in a big clump back into the washing-up bowl, which was also disappointing. But again, it wasn't really as there was nothing to prevent you repeating the process, scooping up the bubbles again and studying them, watching them pop, etc., or was there? Yes, there was – time! Washing-up is so blinking time-consuming! The number of evenings I used to miss something good on telly because I was taking so long washing up.

———————

John's Explanatory Note: I missed seeing Rod Hull's emu attack Michael Parkinson on the telly one Saturday night when I was a young man as I was stuck doing the washing-up, and in a reverie watching the bubbles pop on my rubber gloves. My parents told me about it the next day, as did all my friends, and I've seen the repeats, obviously, but it's not the same – I SO wished I'd been there to witness the assault as it actually happened. (Not that I could have done anything to protect Michael from that stupid, unpredictable bird!)

———————

Dishwasher versus dishcloth

I reckon I take a bit longer to wash up than most because when I've finished the washing-up I like to thoroughly clean the sink and the outside surfaces of the washing-up bowl, which can attract a heck of a lot of grease and grime. I'll turn it upside down and squirt washing-up liquid onto it, and then with a scourer vigorously rub in the detergent and watch the grease on the bottom of the bowl break down and disappear for ever. It's very satisfying. In fact, if you can think of anything more satisfying in life than that, I'd like to hear about it!

Ooh, hang on... I've just thought of something more satisfying: plunging your hands into a washing up bowl of piping hot water, safe in the knowledge that your fleecy yellow gloves will protect you. That's incredibly satisfying, don't you think? Having said that, when the rubber splits in one of the glove fingers, and then hot water floods in all over your hands, but you're not aware until after you've finished washing up when you discover your fingers are all shrivelled up – that's not very satisfying at all!

Although it can take you all night to do the dishes by hand, at least you can tell when the dishes are clean. Sometimes with a dishwasher you can't tell, especially if you've left your specs upstairs. Having said that, wearing spectacles to inspect a completed wash can be disastrous, if the door is opened too soon. The hot air will rush out, steaming up your glasses and reducing visibility to zero. It's wise to have a friend or neighbour standing by to guide you back to your chair so you can defog your lenses in a safe zone. Never try to do it next to the open dishwasher door – you'll be wiping the steam off your glasses all night!

Earlier, I put my dirty cereal bowl in the dishwasher, thinking that all the other dishes in there were also dirty, and that the dishwasher door was left open because it was time for it to go on. But I made a grave error – they weren't dirty, they were spotlessly clean! Clearly Mary had popped the door open to encourage me to empty the dishwasher, but the absence of steam caused me to misconstrue. And now they're dirty again, soiled by dripping milk and cereal residue that has dripped down from my dirty bowl onto all the clean items. For me, this presents a tricky dilemma:

A. Do I locate the soiled items, give them a quick rinse under the tap, then buff them dry with a tea towel, before stacking them

73

away on the shelves along with the items in the dishwasher that were untouched by my dripping milk?

B. Do I put all the dishes through again on the 'fast cycle', which is what Mary would insist on if she found out? What would YOU do, readers?

Oof, I can hear Mary coming out of the lounge so I'll choose option C – shut the dishwasher door and hope it looks like I've emptied the dishwasher already.

"Oh hello, Mary," I say, breezily.

"Thanks for emptying the dishwasher," says Mary, going to put her mug in the 'empty' dishwasher.

"Oh, you're welcome, love, and I'll just take your dirty mug from you, THANK YOU!" I say, swiftly intercepting Mary's mug. "Are you ready to go shopping now, love?"

"I was, but I've just realised... *The Sheriffs Are Coming* is on now," Mary replies, "so let me just watch a few minutes of that while I brush my hair. Don't bother hoovering the lounge. Just do the hall and landing for now, please."

"Yes, why not, Mary? Good idea."

Mary goes in to the lounge, leaving me to abandon option C and choose option B (the 'fast cycle'), which I reckon is the safest option. I'd better do the hoovering now as it should throw up some interesting dilemmas, although I can't think of any at the moment... Oh yes, here's one:

Should you laboriously unwind the whole vacuum-cleaner lead and risk tripping over it continually, or just a bit of it but risk not getting far enough with the cleaner before the fully stretched lead yanks the plug out?

Well, you should unwind the whole lead, of course, and as you move about the room with your vacuum cleaner, repeatedly coil any spare flex into a smallish 'O' so as to minimise the risk of it becoming a safety hazard and getting caught under the hoover as you operate it. That was rather obvious, I think you'll agree, and yet it's distressing to think how many of you will almost certainly ignore the advice I've just given you!

I'd like to catch a bit of *The Sheriffs* before we go shopping so if you don't mind I'm going to end this chapter with a song about a rather harrowing incident that occurred a good few years ago. It's the story of how Mary left me – the only time she ever has done, and I sincerely hope it remains the only occasion!

HAVE YOU SEEN MY WIFE?

There was a time a good few years ago when we didn't own a vacuum cleaner, due to financial restraints. And one day my wife, Mary, said to me, she said, "John, we need a vacuum cleaner." I said, "We can't afford one, love. It's a luxury item." And she left me... she did. And I went into the street looking for her. I said:

"Hey, have you seen my wife?"
I said, "Hey-hey! Have you seen her?
She left me after a row
It was over a vacuum cleaner"
I said, "What's wrong with a broom?"
And she said something obscener
Oh Mary, please come back
and I'll buy you a vacuum cleaner

But she didn't come back, and she wasn't at her sister's in Ashton under Lyne. I didn't know where she was. I had two young children to feed, and to clothe, you know. It was a terrible time. And I asked at the butchers, the bakers – not the candlestick makers, obviously, cos they don't have them any more, do they? I even put out a request on local radio. I said:

75

"Hey, have you seen my wife?"
I said, "Hey-hey! Have you seen her?
She left me after a row
It was over a vacuum cleaner"
I said, "What's wrong with a broom?"
And she said something obscener
Oh Mary, please come back
And I'll buy you a vacuum cleaner

Please come back, Mary. You know, you're right. A broom is not adequate to clean up dog hairs and scraps of unwanted food. Come back and I'll buy you a hoover.

"Hey, have you seen my wife?"
I said, "Hey-hey! Have you seen her?
She left me after a row
It was over a vacuum cleaner"
I said, "What's wrong with a broom?"
And she said something obscener
Oh Mary, please come back
And I'll buy you a vacuum cleaner

Well, I'm delighted to report that she did return. And I bought her a second-hand cylinder model, although we've had a few since then. Mary wants a Dyson now, but I'm not so sure – well, you can see right through them, can't you!

My favourite vacuum cleaner was an Electrolux Glider, which I still have in the garage to hoover up sawdust after carpentry jobs, but it makes a bit of a racket so I guess I have to accept it won't be coming back into the lounge anytime soon.

But I am – to watch a bit of daytime telly with my wife. I'll rejoin you shortly, readers!

CHAPTER 8:

TOO EARLY FOR A LATE (AND OTHER COFFEE QUANDARIES)

I guess you hoped we'd be at the shops by now. I'm terribly sorry but we're still at home, because blinkin' Mary has decided she needs another coffee to help her unwind from all the excitement of this morning's telly! I'm joining her in having an instant because I'm a little hot and bothered myself. Firstly, I did a lot of hoovering, and also certain pre-shopping checks can introduce tension, which makes you crave a hot beverage.

What pre-shopping checks introduce tension?

There's a good few. As well as selecting the appropriate carrier bags, you have to make sure you've got a pound coin for your supermarket trolley. You may need to pop the dog outside (so it can make itself comfortable), as you don't want any accidents in the house while you're out. You must check your kitchen bin and empty if necessary, otherwise bad smells may fester in your absence. If you've been wearing your slippers (highly likely), you must now swap them for an outdoor shoe, and do your laces up, unless you wear a slip-on Cuban heel boot like Ken Worthington, and these activities require another sit-down on the settee to change them. Then it's hard to get up again, but you have to – to make the coffee you're craving. So – a lot of tension! And here comes yet another dilemma: what kind of coffee should you choose? An instant or the cafetiery?

John's Explanatory Note: We'll save the posh coffee dilemmas until we're out at the shops, shall we? Let's just concentrate for now on the types of coffee that are generally available at home: the 'instant' and the 'cafetiery'. Ken Worthington insists it's really spelt 'cafetière' but that doesn't seem right to me – it's 'cafetiery', surely?

What is the cafetiery and why was it invented?

Oof, I really can't answer the second part of that question as I don't think it should have been, and can't fathom why anyone would dream of inventing such a crazy contraption. But it's not my job to prejudge, just to present you with the facts so you can decide for yourselves if the cafetiery is a load of rubbish or not. I'll do my best to give you a potted history of when the cafetiery was invented etc. Erm… in the early nineties, I think, yes, I think it appeared round about that time. And when it first arrived on the scene it was like shower gel all over again – people were very wary of the cafetiery, and justifiably so. The plunger reminded you of a big steam-engine piston, although obviously on a much smaller scale, and the piston enclosure was not cast iron but a glass tube, and it operated vertically, not on its side, and it was coffee, not steam, that was produced – so not very similar at all really!

A family who have used the cafetiery speaks out!

Me and Mary gave the cafetiery a try, we kept an open mind, but I'm afraid when that plunger continually gets stuck in the glass tube, and no amount of effort will push it down through the coffee, and when two of you have finally managed to push it down but the coffee spurts up the sides, over the top and onto your leisure shirt, and Mary's blouse, plus a fleece I think she might have been wearing on that occasion, then you realise the cafetiery is a dreadful invention. That's what happened to us, so we put it back in the box (after washing it out thoroughly) and shoved it at the back of the cupboard, where it has remained ever since. We could give it to the charity shop, but that would be irresponsible – piling misery and heartache onto somebody else. Far better to keep it stored away until a safe solution for its disposal has been thought of by the local council. (A bit like radioactive waste? Yes, not a bad comparison!)

An 'instant' decision

After I'd towelled myself down and Mary had changed her top, we put the kettle on and made ourselves an instant coffee. That's right – we went back to Mellow Bird's, and I suggest you do the same, readers, because you know where you are with an instant. I hope I've said enough to persuade you there really is no point in trying to look swanky and impress your friends by using the cafetiery – your laundry bills will be astronomical, and your quality of life will suffer. Ironic, isn't it, since that's what you were trying to improve by giving that silly contraption a try. Well, you've tried it – now put it back in the box and forget about it, and have an instant. Dilemma over!

Coffee substitutes

Ken Worthington has been known to have – instead of coffee, or hot chocolate (I forgot about that one – mmm, lovely!), a mid-morning Malibu. I really don't advise this, as you're likely to become sluggish and ill prepared to tackle DIY jobs like mowing the lawn if it brightens up a bit. (See Chapter 15: THE LAWN NEEDS MOWING, BUT I NEED A NAP.) Equally, you may develop a loose tongue in your head and say something you regret, like Ken did once when I mentioned there were unsightly weeds peeping out between his patio slabs. He said, "At least there's something growing in my garden!" – a snide reference to the fact that we had our lawn concreted over a while back to create a pleasant maintenance-free space for all the family to enjoy. Sometimes Ken has another tot of Malibu in the early evening before he goes to pick up a takeaway curry. This, Ken maintains, is to steady his nerves as he enters the restaurant, where often young families and courting couples are eating, causing Ken to feel self-conscious as he orders his 'meal for one'.

Once Ken enjoyed a Malibu at Christmas time, except he didn't enjoy it – it made him maudlin. While I wait for the kettle to boil, let me sing a song I wrote in which I tried to put myself in Ken's position, and feel his pain at being alone at Christmas. Please try and imagine Ken's voice singing it (quite high-pitched and croaky, with a poor command of vibrato):

LIFE IS LIKE A MALIBU GLASS

Life is like a Malibu glass
And right now mine is empty
So I fill it up
And toast my luck
For now my life holds plenty
Yes, I'm hopeful
That this old fool
Can drink himself out of this mess
"Cheers, Ken!"
And to all drinking men
"Merry Christmas!"

When I look into my Malibu glass
I see two sad eyes reflected
And in the midst
A cube of ice sits
Where my nose would be expected
Still, I'm certain
When the ice melts
My nose will be resurrected
"Cheers, Ken!"
And to all drinking men
"Merry Christmas!"

"What are you singing about Christmas for, John?" asks Mary, entering the kitchen. "I thought you were making me a coffee!"

"It's coming, Mary," I reply, "just as soon as the kettle's boiled."

"Well, in order for it to boil, you have to switch it on," says Mary, sarcastically.

I touch the kettle and realise it's lukewarm – I've been so busy dealing with domestic dilemmas, I forgot to switch it on!

"Come on, I'll let you buy me a cappuccino in the arcade!" exclaims Mary, generously, "as long as you promise to stop talking to yourself all the time!"

Although Mary pronounced the name of the popular Italian coffee with its luxurious frothy finish incorrectly, as so many do – it's 'campacinno', surely? – I'd be a fool to reject such a generous offer, so I pick up my car keys and shopping bags, check I have a pound coin in the pocket of my fawn slacks, and Mary and I quit the premises and head off in my Austin Ambassador (Y Reg) to the shopping arcade.

And here she is – my beloved Austin Ambassador. Noticing my clenched fist upon the boot, some readers may worry that I'm attempting to scratch the car's paintwork, but that's ridiculous – I was doing nothing of the sort!

Posh coffee dilemmas

Well, we finally made it out of the house, parked the car in the supermarket carpark and walked to the arcade where our first dilemma is how to avoid a coffee shop that is still under construction! They all seem to be like that nowadays – haven't you noticed? – and it's a crying shame that so many are never finished to a satisfactory standard. There's one that's particularly bad: on the ceiling are exposed metal air ducts and the walls have bare brickwork showing. It looks absolutely dreadful and twice I've given the lass on the till the number of a local plasterer who I'm sure would be happy to provide them with a quote, but both times she's looked at me blankly. They could afford the repairs, I'm sure, as the coffee is ever so pricey.

There's a big dopey lad who works there, but to be fair, despite looking dopey, he makes your coffee at lightning speed. He has his headphones on as he works away (ah, maybe he's receiving detailed instructions – I hadn't thought of that!). But I do admire the way he taps the spent coffee grounds out of that thingy with a handle, though it makes such a loud bang – could he do it a bit more gently perhaps? – and the way he cleans the steam nozzle with his little rag while he stares into the distance and sniffs is impressive.

But today we're not going there, we're visiting a long-established coffee shop in the arcade that has no bare brickwork or exposed air ducts. I've just arrived and I'm pleased to note it's got a proper artexed ceiling with traditional beams glued on (clever!), and on the wall there's a lovely photo of two sheepdogs looking the same way, and on another wall a lovely photo of a horse pulling a plough, although there's a bird on its back hindering its progress. I'm hoping to get Mary nice and relaxed here – purchasing her a tiffin to accompany her coffee should help achieve this state – and then extract from her valuable inside tips on all manner of domestic dilemmas that will help make my book a massive best-seller!

The only problem is: Mary has arranged for a friend and a colleague to join us here (erm... just one person, I mean it's a friendly colleague) and she goes by the name of Joan Chitty. I've spoken already about Joan and pretty soon you'll actually get to meet her (I hope you're prepared, readers!). The plan is for Joan to rendezvous with Mary and myself at the cafe – as I've already stated – but Mary has thrown a spanner in the works by nipping to the local chemists to buy some sweeteners while I'm left to greet Joan alone. How will I recognise her? How will she recognise me? Don't worry – we've known each other a long, long time, and besides, Joan has a loud raspy voice, so even if when she arrives I have my head down (cleaning my spectacles with a microfibre lens cloth, perhaps?), then I will know Joan is in the building.

Who exactly is Joan Chitty?

That's a very direct question, if you don't mind me saying, and I'm not sure I'm qualified to answer it! All I can tell you is what you already know – that Joan Chitty works alongside Mary at a local primary school as a dinner lady. For years while Mary was on mixed veg – an important central position which she still holds – Joan was on custard. But in recent years Joan's job has been to break up scuffles in the dinner queue. Well, as I said before, to anticipate them ideally, of course – that's the dream, but will it ever come true? It's my view that Joan, being an asthmatic, should really be back on custard because you've only got to stand and lift your arm up and down, and swivel your wrist a bit, I suppose. Oof, I've just remembered – Joan has weak wrists as well, so that's probably why she's no longer on custard, because a big metal jug full of custard must be heavy. It also explains why Joan's attempts at a career switch a few years ago failed miserably. Joan attended evening classes to train as a physiotherapist, but although she qualified, she never got to practise her new skill, because of her weak wrists.

A candid description of Joan Chitty's lounge

I thought it would be nice to discuss Joan's lounge while I wait for her and Mary, because I do enjoy sitting in there and it's something Mary and I do on a regular basis, usually after I've picked up both ladies from the leisure centre following their exercise class – Bums, Tums and Thighs, or occasionally – Fatburn Extreme. That sounds like a video nasty, doesn't it, readers, but it's not – apparently, it's a class that's been approved by the local council! We sit in Joan's lounge and have an instant, or Mary and Joan might have a glass of white wine while I enjoy a beaker of fruit cordial, and I always sit by the window keeping a close eye on my vehicle parked outside, because it's a little bit rough round where Joan lives. In this position I have a double radiator right next to my legs, which in winter is comforting, and I've noticed the heat is nice and evenly spread so the radiator appears not to require bleeding.

John's Explanatory Note: Worryingly, there is no Allen key on a little loop of string affixed to the radiator, and when enquiries have been made to Joan about her Allen key's whereabouts, she's given me the highly unsatisfactory answer of, "Look, it's somewhere, John, now have another biscuit!"

That reference to biscuits has pre-empted what I was about to say: on the window sill will sit a large plate of assorted biscuits: custard creams, rich tea, fig rolls and occasionally, chocolate Hobnobs! If truth be known I'd rather have the plate on the arm of my chair so I don't have to stretch but Joan worries that it will tumble and the fragile biscuits snap, creating crumbs on the carpet necessitating a cleanup operation, which only happened once but Joan was furious as she hoovered all around my chair. I've never seen her quite so angry. I remained in the chair with my legs lifted up, which is a difficult position to maintain, although my understanding is it's a common position adopted in Pilates, is that right, readers? Ooh I've just got to tell you a sad story about Ken, and then I'll come back to describing Joan's lounge...

Ken's Pilates lady – a tragic love story

Ken Worthington confided in me recently that a couple of years ago he attended (for one month only) a Pilates class, upstairs at the local library, and he became rather taken by a younger woman called Hillary in her early fifties. (I hope I've got her name right, although it's not crucial to the story if the name's wrong, but still it's nice to know.) Ken used to chat to her at the end of the class and eventually he plucked up courage to ask her on a date. But Hillary declined and was honest, saying she didn't fancy Ken, but could they just be friends? Ken was naturally upset, but he accepted that. A couple of weeks later after the class, Hillary told Ken she thought he would be well suited as a boyfriend for her mother, who had been widowed for several years. So a few days later, Ken met her mother (I've got no idea what her name is, but let's call her Pam, shall we?) on a date in a local cafe, but unfortunately Pam didn't fancy Ken either. Awful story, very sad – there are no winners here, only losers, because as far as I know all three people are still single. I'm sorry, I shouldn't have told that story. It just highlights what a sad place the world can be, and reminds me of how lucky I am to be in a secure, loving relationship with Mary.

Joan's lounge (continued)

Still no sign of Mary – or Joan, for that matter. Good – I can finish describing Joan's lounge. On her window sill is a lovely ornament. It's an antelope with its head thrown right back which, although eye-catching, doesn't look quite right to me. It seems like the antelope's horns are about to pierce its own back, which can't be normal antelope behaviour. I'm guessing it was carved by an African tribesman, but Joan bought it in Blackpool so it must have travelled there by sea.

I also enjoy looking at Joan's fish tank. Joan used to have a budgie called Les but, sadly, he died – I might tell you about that in a song a bit later on. Annoyingly, just as I start to admire the fish, Mary always asks me to go and get her handbag from the kitchen because she needs a packet of tissues or her sweeteners, or something else in the bag she requires. I don't mind doing that – it's a husband's duty and what I signed up for when I agreed to marry Mary, I accept that – but I don't know why she can never go and fetch the bag herself, or bring it with her into the lounge? I really hate having to drag myself away from the cosy chair, the radiator and the plate of biscuits, the antelope, monitoring my car outside, and of course looking at the fish and watching them swim through the hole in the rock.

John's Explanatory Note: This hole was not made through natural erosion, I suspect, but in a factory in China. I like it all the more for that, and the fish seem to appreciate it too!

Which posh coffee is best then?

I'm afraid I've no idea… There's the campacinno, which I've already mentioned. That's very nice but a bit 'old hat' nowadays, and while imbibing there's a risk of froth and choco dust being deposited on your upper lip. Mary and I prefer the new one, which I believe is called 'late' (I'm not sure why because it seems to come just as quickly as the others). There's also the 'Americanio', which I first sampled in the cafe of a Heavy Horse Centre in Ashby de la Zouch in 2005. There's another one with hot chocolate in and that's got a funny name. Is it 'Mockery'? Something like that. Try that one if you wish. Try them all if you've money to burn, but I'd advise you not to buy the one that seems very poor value – it's presented in a tiny cup and looks like you've got a bit of brown sludge in the bottom. 'Expressio', that's the one. Extremely bitter, I would imagine, and requiring lots of spoonfuls of sugar.

"Hiya John!" cries a familiar voice.

"It's Joan Chitty!" I reply. "Very nice to see you, Joan."

"Very nice to see you too, John," replies Joan. "Are you on your own?"

"Indeed I'm not, Joan. Mary has just popped to the chemist to buy some sweeteners."

"Has she?" says Joan, chuckling, although to be honest I can't see what's remotely funny about someone going to buy a tube of sweeteners from a chemist, can you, readers?

"Ah, well, we can have a bit of private time then, can't we?" says Joan, sitting down in a chair I'd earmarked for Mary, before continuing, "You're looking very handsome in your new fleece. Look, I'm wearing a new fleece an' all."

"So I see, Joan," I say, and add anxiously, "and I'd love for nothing more than to be able to talk about our fleeces in detail, but right now we need to discuss 'different types of coffee'."

"Oh, I see, why's that, then?" says Joan, looking puzzled.

I suddenly remember how knowing I was writing a book made Mary clam up, so in case Joan reacts the same way it might be best not to tell her too much at this stage. However, I'm hoping that as an experienced dinner lady (though no longer on custard), Joan will drop me the occasional nugget without realising, just in passing conversation. I decide to change the subject.

"I'd have thought Mary would be here by now, Joan, but she's obviously still at the chemists – in a queue for the till, stuck behind someone wanting advice perhaps about a nasal spray?"

"Ooh, how do you know that?" says Joan, as if she's just seen a magician do a clever trick.

"I don't, Joan. But it's possible," I reply, rationally. "And if it were the case, and the assistant thinks it wise that they have a word with the pharmacist before they process the nasal spray transaction, but the pharmacist is currently busy helping other customers, and then when he or she is finally free, they have to ask the lady or gentleman customer a few questions about who the nasal spray is for and whether or not they're allergic to certain drugs, and then the customer decides – depending on the pharmacist's advice – to choose a different nasal spray, which will require the pharmacist to ask more questions, well, Mary will be kept waiting. And what if Mary is stuck behind two or even three such customers, Joan? She might not get here for hours!"

"She might find her coffee's gone cold. I'd better drink it," says Joan, picking up a coffee cup left by a previous customer.

"Ooh, you'd better not, Joan!"

"Ugh, that's cold already!" gasps Joan, putting down the cup hurriedly. "Why didn't you warn me, John?"

"I DID try to warn you, Joan, but you were too quick for me. Our coffee has yet to arrive. I think they're a bit short-staffed today, so that's why that cup wasn't cleared away... oof!"

"Oh, dearie me!" says Joan, wiping her mouth with a tissue. "I might be ill now. Why don't you go and tell the waitress to hurry up, John, and to come and clear this table!"

"I will do, Joan," I continue, frowning slightly. "The thing is – I ordered a 'late' for both Mary and myself, and I'm just wondering if that's why they're called that, after all? I always assumed they came as quickly as the others, but in view of our long wait I'm beginning to think now that was perhaps a bit stupid of me."

"Well, I don't know what to say to that, John," says Joan, struggling to take her fleece off before draping it over the back of Mary's chair.

"It's a dilemma, though, isn't it?" I ask Joan, probingly, but she doesn't respond. Joan is now busy on her mobile phone chuckling at a photo somebody's just sent her – I presume. I did just hear it go 'ping'.

"I'll go and see what's happened to the coffees," I say finally, getting up, "and, of course, order a coffee for YOU, Joan. What type would you prefer? Take your time in deciding, and feel free to discuss any dilemmas you feel you're facing as you make your choice."

"Ooh, yes I will," replies Joan. "Erm… can I have a full-fat Machiatto, please, duck?" says Joan, with a sophisticated smile.

Oof, there's quite a big queue now, so while I wait to buy Joan a coffee (and find out what's happened to ours), why don't I sing a little song I wrote all about her to celebrate her qualifying as a physio, which, as I've already stated, she did a few years ago.

When I wrote it, I performed it on my organ to Joan in her lounge, and I noticed she had tears streaming down her cheeks as I sang. I assumed at the time it was because she was so happy at having a song written for her, but with hindsight it must have been because she was sad, knowing her weak wrists would prevent her from ever kneading and pummelling a client's body.

Still, let's now imagine Joan has sturdy wrists and a bright future ahead as a physio, while I sing the song (quietly, as the person in front of me in the queue keeps turning round to see what I'm whispering about!).

CONGRATULATIONS JOAN

Congratulations Joan
Congratulations Joan
No more working as a dinner lady
Lumpy custard, greasy gravy
Come on – get on your throne
Congratulations Joan
You no longer have cause to moan
Erm... Your stature has considerably grown
With you no one will ever dare pick a bone!

I can't remember any more lines, sorry. But as you can see, it contains a lot of rhymes with 'Joan'. It's a 'feelgood' number that works best with a stomping disco beat. As I said to Ken, I'm convinced a young dance troupe could have a field day with it, as long as they put the work required into rehearsing it. Anyway, Joan didn't become a physio – she's still a dinner lady and I'm nearly at the front of the queue. Oof, what was that funny coffee she asked for? I've forgotten...

Ah, Mary's now back, I see, sitting talking to Joan. Hang on, they're both sipping coffee. Ours must have arrived, but that means Joan's drinking mine. Oof! Charmed, I'm sure! I'll have to drink hers now with the funny name that I can't remember. Hmm, maybe I'll just order another late...

White, brown or are you sweet enough?

Mary's sweet enough, obviously, and that's why she doesn't take sugar. Nevertheless, she does like to pop a sweetener in her hot drinks, hence her visit to the chemist. Mary dispenses it into her drink with a single click if she wants one sweetener, which she tends to these days. She used to click it twice when she had a sweeter tooth, as we all did a few years back, didn't we, readers?

I used to have three sugars in my tea when I was a lad, and my father Bernard had five! I loved watching him spoon it into his teacup, and after he'd popped in the fifth spoonful, he'd turn to me and do a big wink before he began the mammoth task of stirring it all in. Ah, happy days! Nowadays I have only half a spoonful of sugar in my tea, and I prefer white, I must say. I know brown's supposed to be healthier for you but I don't see how it can be – it's unrefined to start with, and the granulated brown sugar looks a lot like cusscuss. Cusscuss? Yes, cusscuss, although it's possible I've not got the spelling quite right this time. It should be spelt like that though, because the product makes you want to swear – at least twice! While I wait for my late, let me tell you a strange and sorry tale…

A Cusscuss calamity

A few years before Ken Worthington picked up his clarinet to begin that fateful performance on *New Faces* in 1973, he was a beatnik (with a finger monkey as a pet, so he claims), living in shared accommodation in the St Helens area. One evening, Ken borrowed a fellow lodger (and beatnik)'s brown sugar and put it in his cup of tea (an earthenware unglazed mug, I'll be bound!). But it wasn't sugar… no, it was blinkin' cusscuss! When Ken told me about that I had to chuckle, but then when I thought about it later I was saddened, for two reasons.

1: Why was the beatnik storing bags of dried wheat, when his shelves could have been crammed with small jars of crab paste, or tins of creamed mushrooms – they were coming through at the time, early seventies, and I used to love them. Surely beatniks and hippies would have done so too?

2: Why was Ken considering putting brown sugar in his tea, anyway, rather than white? Wasn't that thought of as a bit dirty at the time? It must to some degree discolour the tea, surely?

Tiffin or chocolate brownie?

Well, I'm sat back down now and Joan and Mary are chatting away about something or other, and they're sharing a second tiffin, which I've just had to buy. (Joan ate up all the first one, which was intended for Mary only!) A few years ago it would have been a doughnut, but it seems the tiffin has captured the nation's hearts – and Joan's too, judging by the way she's tucking into it. Oof, I'm not buying a third one...

Let's backtrack a little. The Great British Public had a long love affair with flapjack in the sixties and seventies, but that oat-and-syrup favourite was sidelined by the arrival of the chocolate brownie in 1987 (I've just guessed that date, but that's roughly when I first became aware of them). However, in recent years the tiffin has gained considerable ground, and to be honest, it's a bit nicer to eat than the brownie, don't you think, readers? The brownie can be a bit claggy and overly moist, especially at the garden centre, but if you go to the till to complain the lady's always out the back reheating someone's soup, so after a while I give up waiting and go back to my seat and eat it anyway.

Ooh, I'd forgotten about the muffin, which is very popular too, but they're overrated, in Mary's view. Privately, I suspect Mary's a bit sore about the fact that muffins now completely overshadow the fairy cake, to the extent that nobody even mentions fairy cakes any more. I've reassured Mary, reminding her that fairy cakes are still going strong at school fetes to raise money for the new minibus, and she'll be pleased that I'm mentioning fairy cakes in this book, which I have done now – four times!

"Ooh, sorry, John!" says Joan suddenly. "I seem to have eaten all of the tiffin. You didn't have a single bite! Would you like me to go and buy you another one?"

"It's fine, Joan," I reply, magnanimously. "I've got a Hobnob wrapped in some foil in my coat pocket from the other day when I was masticking the bathroom window sill. I was up a ladder and not sure how long I'd be there, so I took provisions."

"Ooh, I see," replies Joan, chuckling, while Mary tuts and looks displeased.

And I eat the Hobnob, though furtively, keeping it hidden in my pocket and breaking off small sections of the biscuit before transferring them from pocket directly to mouth, while checking to see that no members of staff are observing me, knowing full well it's highly illegal to eat your own food on commercial premises.

CHAPTER 9:

LET'S GO SHOPPING!

Very well, yes, we can. Because we've finished our coffee and said goodbye to Joan Chitty, who has an appointment at the doctor's to have her blood pressure taken.

John's Explanatory Note: Joan is actually going to see the nurse, but if I'd said, "Joan has an appointment at the nurse's", you'd have thought I was a bit odd. But as more and more appointments nowadays ARE with the nurse instead of the doctor, perhaps it's only a matter of time before that expression slips into common usage.

Joan is a lucky lady, in my view, having her blood pressure taken. It's so exciting when they wrap that thing that pumps up around your arm and you have to be still and quiet while they check you. Then there's genuine tension as you watch the numbers on the

95

monitor decrease and there's a click, before the air comes out, and you glance at the nurse to see if they're looking worried, but they always have their face turned away so you've no idea what's going on! Then there's a satisfying ripping sound as the Velcro fastening is released and they say, "You'll live!" Ooh, I can't wait for my next one!

Meanwhile, me and Mary are going to the supermarket, finally! Some of you may be wondering: as you're in the arcade already, isn't there a dilemma about whether you should first get a key cut? Well spotted, those of you who thought that, and normally I'd agree. But we don't need one cutting at the moment, thank you. Shame really, because while you're waiting for your key to be cut you can check out belt and holdall prices on the next stall!

One day, I suspect supermarkets will provide a key-cutting service, at which point we need never visit the arcade again, although that would be a shame as the pound shop's there and I like to buy a large tube of family toothpaste every now and again. Mary's not requested that I do that – it's just my way of contributing to the family's dental welfare and it reinforces that I'm the man of the house, doing that. I just like coming home and plonking a large tube of Ultrabrite on the table. But then Mary says, "Put it the bathroom cabinet, John!", so then I do that.

John's Explanatory Note: In Stone Age times it would have been a mammoth I'd have brought back for the family to share. Mind you, they'd have been too big to carry, so maybe a wild boar or just a rabbit even?

While we're on the subject of toothpaste (and we'll be discussing tooth-brushing dilemmas later in the book, of course), have you noticed how many shops now stock tubes of toothpaste: the chemist, the garage, the hardware shop, the pound shop, not to mention the supermarket, and it's becoming a dilemma trying to decide which store to buy it from. They've even started selling it at our dentist's! Mind you, it's a bit pricey there, so I tend not to bother, preferring to spend my time waiting for my appointment in pouring myself a cooling cup of complimentary drinking water from the dispenser. If you have several cupfuls (and I generally do), you may be lucky enough to witness a giant bubble force itself from the bottom of the bottle, as air rushes from outside to equalise the lower air pressure inside the bottle.

"John, what ARE you gabbling on about?" Mary asks, with a sigh.

"Nothing much, love," I reply, realising we've arrived at the supermarket. "Ooh, we're here!"

"Pound coin, please!"

This is a moment I love: removing the pound coin from my bumbag. There may be a brief hiatus while I mistakenly pass Mary a 10p piece, but her tutting will alert me to the fact that I got the wrong coinage and the error will be swiftly rectified, before the pound coin is inserted in a (medium-sized) trolley and separated by yours truly from the other trolleys. I generally operate the trolley throughout our shopping trip – I've the height and upper-body strength to manoeuvre it safely and make sudden direction changes if required, while Mary walks slightly ahead, although wouldn't it be safer if she walked behind? Hmm, this brings us to our first supermarket dilemma!

Should the trolley operator walk in front or behind?

John's Explanatory Note: This applies only to those out shopping in couples or family groups. Those shopping alone (like

Ken Worthington) need not concern themselves with this dilemma, and they probably only need a small basket, anyway.

> In front: there's a risk of them rushing ahead and losing contact with the other person, who may have stopped while they search for the crab paste (always difficult to locate), and it could be several minutes before the two parties reconvene in a different aisle, and when you do so the mood of the person you left behind may have somewhat deteriorated.

> Behind: the partner in front may stop suddenly to consider the freshness of a pineapple, while the one with the trolley – drawn perhaps to the colourful Sugar Puffs promotion up ahead, and not noticing that the person in front has stopped – will crash into them, the trolley catching them on the heel, and inflicting a blow as painful as that endured when you bash your shin on the dishwasher door!

Naturally, I will take great care as I follow Mary with the trolley. Oops... I nearly failed to notice that she stopped then to pick up a bag of Jersey Royals, but hopefully she'll remember that we've loads of spuds and put them back and move on... which she has, lovely! But now she's stopped again... aha, she's bumped into Linda from the halfway house (where I used to cut the grass and I'm sure I'll be mentioning that in a later chapter when we get on to DIY dilemmas). They seem deeply engrossed in conversation, so I reckon I've time to sing another song, all about regional differences in the shopping experience.

This one has a rollicking, tub-thumping quality. It could be sung by a group of friends who have met up for a school reunion, or equally by a party of sales reps (on a trust-building course) in the foyer of a Travel Lodge. Ooh no, they're quite tiny – Travel Lodge foyers – so I suggest they sing it in the Harvesters next door, or even outside in the carpark.

SHOPKEEPERS IN THE NORTH

When I go shopping in the north I find
The service is always splendid
A cheery smile you can count on while
The right change is being tendered

If anyone dares criticise their wares
They never will be offended
If it needs repairs they'll even lend you theirs
While yours is being mended

Shopkeepers in the north are nice
They ask after your kids and wife
And when you've had a good chinwag
They pop your provisions in your bag

But when I go shopping in London Town
Why do they act so haughty?
Standing there with their nose in the air
As if you've done something naughty

My "how-do-you-do?" in the chip-shop queue
Was received in total silence
My "take care, cock!" in the butcher's shop
Was met with a look of violence...

I'm sure most shopkeepers in London are nice really, but I've always suspected people get nicer the further north you travel. But I wasn't sure about this – I needed proof. So a few years ago I made a feature film to test the theory called *It's Nice Up North*. It was extremely popular, so much so that it went straight to DVD! An internationally renowned stills photographer called Martin Parr filmed it, but he was quite wobbly with the camera (surprising for a 'stills' photographer), and I've since decided he can't be that good, as not only does he not do weddings, he hasn't even got a shop! We travelled up to the Shetland Isles and proved the theory, although probably the nicest person we met came from Devon, which was a bit unfortunate. So the theory is um, well… not proven really.

And the trip to the Shetland Isles was made in the nicest of motor vehicles – my Y Reg! Yes, it did break down – but once repaired it got me safely home again. No wonder I'm looking slightly smug!

A trip to the North Pole (will it be nice?)

Mary and I have split up. Oof, I don't mean we're getting a divorce, I mean she's gone in search of a kettle-fur stopper – a task I would have much preferred to the one I've been given: finding a jar of 'pestio'. Our Karen's coming home at the weekend for a visit with her flatmate Maxine and they both like it cos they've both gone veggie, but as I've previously stated, it looks to me like someone's filled a jar with mould and resealed the lid. How can they be allowed to do that? Perhaps I shouldn't be too hasty to condemn. I remember we were very wary of that pink stuff, taramasaladata, I believe it's called? But now Mary and I eat it with confidence along with some of Peter's bread — lovely!

In the old days if you couldn't find something at the supermarket you had to wander helplessly on your own until you stumbled upon the item hours later, or just gave up and went home. All that has changed, as nowadays the store assistant is legally bound to accompany you to the precise location of the item you're after, and point to it. They can't just say: "It's over there — in the second aisle along next to the cream crackers." If they did that, they'd be sacked, and rightfully so. Once you've informed them of the item you're seeking, you must follow them on a long journey, and sometimes — if it's a big store and the item is many aisles away — it feels like you're going on an expedition with them.

And that's happening now. Whilst I can't pretend I'm not anxious, I'm also slightly excited. This mood is heightened by the temperature changes experienced as you pass from the warmth of the Bakery to the Chilled Foods section, where obviously the temperature plummets. If you close your eyes — not a good idea as you might bump into someone pushing their trolley — you can imagine your expedition is from the Tropics to the North Pole, and you might worry that you're not suitably attired. But don't fret too much. When you arrive at Chilled Foods the freezing draught blowing from the cabinets is offset by hot-air blowers from above to warm you up again — fantastic!

John's Explanatory Note: Isn't it clever of modern super-markets to mimic the atmospheric conditions of today's natural world? Because, you know, I've heard it's getting quite warm up there at the North Pole, which is melting the ice, so the polar bears have nothing to stand on. Having said that, might the warmer air stop them shivering with their depleted body fats as they try to hunt for the fish that are no longer there? Ooh, it's a tricky one!

———————

Although your instinct may be to chat to the assistant and get to know them better during the long journey together, they tend to walk ahead of you in silence. This is my shopping experience today. It's quite normal and you mustn't feel slighted. Chances are they'll have a microphone headset on (mine certainly has, along with a stylish baseball cap), and this is in case they get a message from security, or Sheila in Wet Fish needs some more ice (like the polar bears do), and I suppose if you get lost on your expedition they can radio for assistance.

But today we're anything but lost. Indeed, it looks as if we've arrived at our destination. Goodness, that was quick! I'd love to shake hands with the lady who's brought me all this way, relive the best bits of the journey with them, even exchange photos via blue teeth – had we taken any, which sadly we haven't, but it's too late – she's gone. Having pointed to the pestio and made sure that I've engaged with the item the shop assistant has begun the long journey back to, well... somewhere else in the supermarket. I wish them well in their future trips with customers around the store.

Which flavour pestio: mould or rust?

I'm taking my time choosing now because it seems there are two types of pestio. One is the green mouldy one that I recognise, and the other is a reddish-brown shade that I've not noticed before. It resembles a jar of rusty metal flakes, like what you would get from rubbing a wire brush for ages against a rusty car exhaust pipe, mixed with peanut butter. Surely they wouldn't do that, would they? Well, yes, if they're prepared to shove mould into a jar, why not bits of rusty metal? I'd better take one jar of each, and let our Karen decide which one she dare risk eating first.

Self-service or manned checkout?

So you've got all your shopping, and it's time to pay for it. But which checkout should you visit? Common sense suggests you should go to the till with a real person manning it, because at least then you know you'll get to chat to a real person that day (a lot of people – especially those who live alone, like Ken Worthington – don't, of course, and have to make do with talking to the TV). How do you know they'll say hello to you at the till? Because legally they HAVE to say hello to you (apart from in Aldi as we've discussed, where you're advised to keep your head down and get packing, but you wouldn't be able to hear each other anyway above all the beeping). They didn't used to be legally bound to say hello to you, but the rule was introduced a few years ago at most supermarket checkouts, and in my view it's helped to make the world a brighter, happier place.

Who should say 'hello' first, you or the checkout person?

This is a very important point! Whatever you do, you MUST wait for the person on the till to say hello before you speak. NEVER EVER say hello until they've said it first. DO YOU UNDERSTAND? Oof, sorry, sounds like I'm getting a bit heavy but I just can't stress this enough. Let them say hello first and your shopping experience will remain pleasant. Break this golden rule and you're in big trouble. You see, readers, once I said hello too soon with dire consequences, and I'm going to tell you all about it now. It's an upsetting story, but I urge you not to shy away from reading it. It will help convince you never to make the same mistake.

The time I said 'hello' too soon

I was shopping alone. Mary had gone to the garden centre with her friend Doreen Melody (the lady with the camper van), and I had been entrusted with the weekly family shop. I had done the shopping, was at the till with my trolley, and was next in line to have my items scanned. As the previous customer (an elderly lady) was slipping her fingers into the handle of her carrier bag, the young lass on the till turned to look at me – I thought! So I said "Hello". But with hindsight I realise she must have been looking right through me – daydreaming perhaps about what she might have done with her life had she not started working at the supermarket? Whatever she was thinking, she wasn't legally bound to begin her next transaction. Indeed, as the old lady hadn't departed, and her shopping bag was still making contact with the till, the lass on the till wasn't even legally permitted to say hello to me, and to have done so could have led to an instant dismissal. But, doh – I didn't know about that rule then. Nobody had told me!

My greeting being met with silence, I was initially baffled and then slightly offended. So I leaned in and said "Excuse me, love – I said 'Hello'." My words may have been lost beneath the screaming of a toddler in the next aisle, I'm not sure, but the lass on the till still didn't respond, just turned her head away and smiled at a male colleague who was folding up some cardboard boxes nearby.

She'd snubbed me twice now, this lass, and two schoolboys behind me started sniggering. I felt utterly humiliated as my understanding was that she was legally bound to say hello to me, followed by the phrase (optional and discretionary) "Do you need any help with your packing today?"

The old lady finally got her fingers into her bag handle and left, and as she did so the assistant turned to me and started scanning my items. She now had no excuses not to say hello to me, but guess what, readers? She said absolutely nothing, and made only the briefest attempt at eye contact, throwing me a funny look, for some reason, before hurriedly looking away again – very rude! It was a miserable moment, and I looked around at the schoolboys and other customers in the queue for sympathy, but they were avoiding eye contact with me too!

―――――――――

John's Explanatory Note: I realise that supermarket customers aren't legally bound to say hello or establish eye contact with each other, but it would have been nice if at this point they had!

―――――――――

I felt utterly alone, and I continued to suffer in silence until the checkout girl had finished scanning my shopping and I was putting the last items in my bag. I leant forward and said, confidentially, "Erm, I presume you're aware you didn't say hello to me, because you ARE legally obliged to, aren't you?" But my mouth had gone dry and it came out really quiet and croaky, and she had her head down in her till counting out some pound coins, so she missed that one as well. Then she turned to me and said in a bright and breezy manner, like everything was hunky dory, "Would you like your receipt, sir?"

I was stunned. This lass, who had been acting like I was a complete stranger, was suddenly behaving like I was a titled gentleman who she had the utmost respect for. Also, she was asking a ridiculous question. Of course I wanted my receipt! How else would I check my items against the bill to ascertain that no errors had been made and I wasn't due a refund? (Considering trust with this particular supermarket employee was non-existent, I knew I would be checking my receipt extremely carefully!)

———————

John's Explanatory Note: Since then I've had the question "Would you like your receipt?" asked loads of times in various stores. It's all to do with saving paper, they'd like you to think, and if so, I applaud that heartily, but is there something more sinister going on? Is it really just a ruse to stop people on their way out, accuse them of shoplifting, then force the embarrassed and 'receiptless' shopper into paying for the items all over again? Hmm, the jury's still out on that one...

———————

Anyway, when she said "Would you like your receipt, sir?" I just shook my head in disbelief at the way I'd been treated, which obviously she took to mean, "No, I wouldn't like my receipt." So, guess what? I didn't get my receipt, so not only could I not check my shopping bill for errors, but I was worried the security man might arrest me on the way out for having no proof of purchase. Thank goodness he was distracted in trying to free some wire baskets that had got stuck together.

Unknown item in the baggage area!

I know it's a machine, but at least you know where you are with the automatic checkout. And although they don't give you much chance to chat, it IS possible to hold a conversation with them. To "Unknown item in the baggage area!" you can reply in a jaunty fashion, "My library book is actually very familiar to me, thank you. In fact, I'm about to renew it for the sixth time!" Maybe you can think of something cleverer than that, but I can't at the moment. Yes, since my awful experience I've tended to put my shopping through the automatic tills. Unless I'm with Mary, as she likes me to lift the heavier items from the trolley onto the conveyor belt – big box powders, kitchen roll multipacks, etc. – before placing them into carrier bags, which Mary is holding steady, and finally lifting the bags back into the trolley.

In the past, my job was to hold the bags steady while Mary placed the items in the bag. But – eager to ascertain that the bag was being correctly loaded – I would be constantly bobbing and weaving my head to maintain a good view of Mary's work in progress. At the same time Mary's head would be moving a fair bit as she lifted and placed the items in the bags, and unfortunately on occasion our heads would collide. This would make Mary absolutely furious, and once she smacked me on the arm of my anorak quite hard, so in the end the system was abandoned, and replaced with the current arrangement.

Perhaps recognising this potential hazard, automatic tills have been designed so each item is loaded into the bag individually. These tills don't usually say hello (after my bad experience I don't mind that!), but they always thank you at the end, and some even say goodbye to you. However, I notice the Coop voice sounds a bit anxious, which can make you anxious yourself, and worry your items won't scan, which, let's face it, they often don't. Beware too of the self-service till in Sainsbury's. I've not heard it myself but according to Ken, it's the voice of a lass who seems friendly enough when you're all done, because she says "Thank you!" in a way that seems like she really is grateful you've done your shopping with the store that day. But then as you're picking up your bags and about to leave, she says (in a very sarcastic voice), "GoodBYE!" Well, it sounds like she can't wait to see the back of you, and leaves you feeling worthless, says Ken. It does seem strange, and maybe that lass needs to learn some manners by listening to the customer announcement in Aldi, which, as I recall, goes something like this:

Dear Customers, we are overjoyed to announce that for your comfort and convenience Till 5 will shortly be opening up just for you!

Now, that's what I call customer service!

Let's end this often fraught and emotional chapter on shopping with a 'feelgood' number I wrote after a trip to the hardware store with Mary. Hopefully, it will restore your faith in the high-street retail experience, and make you realise shopping really can be a whole lot of fun!

THE HARDWARE STORE

I have come to the hardware store
Looking for household cleaners
With my wife though presently
There's an aisle that lies between us
For she's in search of laundry liquid
And my quest is for bleach
I stop to assist
A lady with a bad wrist
Get a duster that's just out of her reach

There's excitement in the air
And a heavy whiff of polish
Bargain products on every shelf
To remain here all day is our wish
Happily this may be granted
For our shopping list is long
And progress is slow
For I keep stopping to
Hear the lovely music they put on

LET'S GO SHOPPING!

It's a place I feel so alive
So happy and secure
So give it a try
You can even buy
Toilet rolls in packs of twenty-four.

I have come to the hardware store
But sadly our trip is over
A cup of tea awaits at home
And a brief sit-down on the sofa
Then the thrill of unpacking the bags
And reliving our recent visit
To the hardware store
Where we'll be back for sure
We forgot the blinkin' laundry liquid!

CHAPTER 10:

GOD BLESS THE FLEECE!

Oof, we're onto Chapter 10 already and I've still not had my dinner! Despite that Hobnob earlier I'm getting decidedly peckish, and there is a dilemma that occurs about now, in between coffee break and dinner time. Do you know what it is? No? Don't worry – this is why I'm here, to teach you and guide you through the day and help you avoid life's pitfalls. Consider me a guru, if you like – but please don't expect me to don a funny gown or sit cross-legged up in a tree, because it's not going to happen – that's dangerous! Anyhow, the dilemma is this: do you wait for your main meal, or have an interim snack to keep you going? A finger of fudge, or if you're environmentally conscious, a Roasted Nut Tracker bar? It's tempting, but no, I think you should wait for your din-dins. Come on, show some strength of character! Have a Locket if you're a bit throaty, or ferret around in your bumbag – why, there may a Victory V waiting for you! Or in your coat pocket some Extra Strong Mints? But please, if any are lying loose and have become discoloured, jettison them immediately – sucking them means a poorly tummy may ensue. Not convinced? Listen to this:

TUMMY TROUBLE

Tummy trouble – prevents you from going outdoors
Tummy trouble – as often as not is caused
By swallowing food too quickly
Without chewing it, particularly
Food that's sweet and sickly, or pickly

That's a snatch of my song, 'Tummy Trouble'. I can't remember any more, I'm afraid, but you get the message.

I mentioned coat pockets a moment ago, which has reminded me of something I discussed in a previous chapter: changing out of your slippers into an outdoor shoe. But, silly me, I forgot to advise on suitable torso protection for the great outdoors – you know, a coat! If, as a result of that omission, I've made you go out shopping without wearing a coat, jacket or fleece, I humbly apologise, and trust that you didn't get too cold?

I'm warm as toast in my fleece, as I sit on a bench outside the public library with all the shopping bags. "Where's Mary gone?" you may be wondering. "Did you not manage to reconvene after your expedition to find the pestio?" We did, thanks for asking, and we managed to fill the shopping bags with items without our heads colliding. But then – just as I was going to ask Mary to discuss the dilemma of which charity bin you should put your blue token in – she received a text from Joan Chitty, who had finished at the nurse's (see – I called it the nurse's, NOT the doctor's!), and Mary dashed off to meet Joan at the dry cleaner's, while I decided to walk down to the library and wait with the shopping.

It's a pleasant yet slightly forlorn spot, here outside the library. I'm sat on the bench – on me tod – with little or no interaction with other members of the public. Those who do pass by seem to have their head down deep in thought or looking for their library card, and they all move slowly as if in a dream. (Not like at the pound shop, where people move jerkily as they grab the bargains – and who can blame them!) Ooh, a pigeon has just landed nearby, and while it's bucking the trend by moving jerkily outside the library that's because that's how just pigeons walk, isn't it? Oof, it's coming towards me, but I can't offer it any food scraps because – as I've already stated – that Hobnob is long gone, and to be fair, it seems like quite a plump pigeon so I'm probably more hungry than they are. What a shame that pigeons and, for that matter, all the birds that we daily feed scraps to don't just occasionally return the favour and drop a paper bag full of sausage rolls into your lap? (Four for £1 at the baker's, you know, which seems to me an incredible offer.) But they're never going to, are they, so we'd better get used to it, I suppose...

Ooh, it's getting a bit cold, so if you don't mind I'm going to do up the zip of my fleece. "What would we do without our fleeces, eh, readers?" If I'd asked you that thirty years ago you'd have looked at me like I'd lost my marbles, because the fleece hadn't been invented then. But in the modern world of uncertainty, the fleece is a beacon of calm and stability, would you not say? When you pop on a fleece and do up the zipper, or slip it on over your head and do up the much shorter zip, or leave the zipper down if you're in a casual mood, why, all seems right with the world. It's a reason to be happy and even sing a little song...

(I'd better sing this one quietly, an' all – I don't want the ladies in the library to think I'm a street drinker, as they do tend to congregate here on a weekday...)

FLEECE THE WORLD

God bless the fleece
It brings you inner peace
I can't conceive of a finer outer garment
I'm surprised that the Police
Haven't championed the fleece
For officers on the beat
Or even the sergeant

Goodbye, fair cagoule
You've been made to look a fool
By a coat superior
In every department
I know you've got a hood
But you're really not as good
And to think my love for you was once so ardent!

So God bless the fleece
It doesn't crumple, it doesn't crease
Of styles and colours there's a huge variety
When sporting a fleece
The plasterer and the priest
Occupy the same high niche
In society

I hope and I pray
That the fleece is here to stay
Like the baseball cap
Which also looks so stylish
If I should lose my fleece
I would not be pleased
So don't attempt to steal it
That would be childish

Oh it's my wish
And my grandniece's
That one day everyone in the world will be wearing fleeces
I'd be thrilled to pieces if it came true
Will it come true?
It's up to you!

I wrote that song a good few years ago, and I'm delighted to note that my dream DID come true – just about everybody in the world is now wearing a fleece. Perhaps not all the time, but certainly when walking the dog or generally 'chillaxing', as I've heard Joan Chitty describe her leisure time. Readers may like to know that I personally own six fleeces – remarkably, the same number as Joan. She did only have four but last month she bought another two in a '2 for 1' sale at Millets. They've gone much thinner in recent years though, haven't they, fleeces, and Joan's are mainly the thin lightweight ones, 'microfleeces', I believe they're called by fleece-industry professionals, so pound for pound I still own more fleeces than Joan cos mine are heavier and have more of a woolly texture. It's not a competition though, is it? Hmm, in a way it is, yes!

Goodbye, fair cagoule!

I feel very sorry for the cagoule, which of late seems to have been sorely neglected by the general public. Having said that, I still see hikers wearing cagoules when I'm at Toad Mouth Rock near Hathersage. I like to park up there, and – while enjoying a leisurely Werther's – try and spot the mouth of the toad, as it's not always apparent when you're driving past. Also, when I'm at the Ladybower reservoir checking the level, cagoule wearers come by in large groups nattering away, and some carry a big stick like that

Ian McKellen had in *Lord of the Rings*. But they're always in far too much of a hurry to be checking the level properly, so what on earth is the point of visiting the reservoir in the first place, I ask you!

I still wear my cagoule – or 'kagoule', as it can be spelt. Ooh, that's a dilemma in itself: cagoule or kagoule? What do you think? I think kagoule looks more racy, so I'll spell it like that from now on, shall I? Yes, sometimes I wear my kagoule over my fleece, because let's face it, the kagoule does something very well that the fleece does poorly – it keeps the rain out. And when it's raining hard and you've got your kagoule hood up, it's like you're in a tent and you can hear the rain drumming. Ooh, it's lovely. So how on earth did the kagoule get usurped by the fleece? Well, the answer is partly contained in the lyrics of the previous song. For a fuller understanding of this perplexing issue we need to look at a type of fruit that was once, like the cagoule... oops, sorry, the kagoule – very popular: the peach.

The big peach/nectarine debate

At one time the peach was the obvious first choice for a piece of fruit – if you didn't fancy an apple, or an orange, or a banana, I suppose. Or a pear? No, in my humble view, pears often disappoint by being too hard and they take far too long to get soft so the public lost confidence in them many years ago. So no, you went for a peach with its silky luxurious skin and juicy interior. Throughout the sixties and seventies the peach reigned supreme.

But then in the early eighties the nectarine was introduced and we had a dilemma: should you buy the less easily bruised nectarine or remain loyal to the easily damaged peach? It was difficult, and it was painful, but gradually loyalties switched to the nectarine. Though having said that, in recent years... I don't know, but I think people aren't that fond of nectarines any more and have gone

It becomes even more difficult to choose between a peach and a nectarine when a jasper ('wasp' to Southern readers) is hovering in the immediate vicinity!

back to the peach. But are we really that bothered about peaches either, now that mangoes have arrived?

Never mind mangoes, or kagoules.. what about the windcheater?

Ooh, now then... I've just remembered about the windcheater and how popular THEY were before kagoules came along. Everyone had a windcheater, or if they didn't, they were jealous of anyone who did (the same was true of duffel bags, to some degree), but then the lightweight kagoule was introduced and people loved it and immediately lost interest in the windcheater. Well, I did, anyway. Except that you couldn't sew a badge on a kagoule very easily. It would risk tearing the fabric. As for an iron-on badge – a kagoule was useless for that. You'd clog up your iron with melted plastic and your wife would be furious. Well, mine was, so how did kagoules overtake windcheaters in popularity? The 'tent in the rain' effect when the hood was up and it was raining, of course! But I do quite miss my windcheater as it had nice toggles on a drawstring coming out of the hood.

John's Explanatory Note: The downside of these toggles on a drawstring is that they could be mistaken for buzzing flies if you were walking quickly – you know, the toggles would jerk about like annoying bluebottles, or even jaspers (wasps – as I've already stated in the photo caption above), in your peripheral vision.

Hmm, if I still had my windcheater I could sew on a few badges I've accrued in recent years, including one for a Butterfly Park near Sutton Coldfield that Mary and I visited in 2009, when a fabulous day was had by all. Well, by me and Mary...

Another negative aspect of the cagoule (note, we've gone back to the 'c' spelling of cagoule because I think I prefer it. It looks a bit nicer – hope that's all right with you, readers?) is the horrible swishing noise they make when you take them off. It's particularly unpleasant to the wearer because it's incredibly loud as you pull the cagoule over your head. (I'm not sure what the decibel level is and presumably it falls within legal limits, but has anyone done a proper test on it?) As it passes your ears it sounds deafening to me!

A trip to the Pencil Museum

I'll always remember visiting the Pencil Museum in Keswick, Cumbria in 2007. It was a very special day, and yes – standing next to the tallest pencil in the world IS a humbling experience. If ever you're feeling too big for your boots, visit the Pencil Museum in Keswick and go and stand next to the tallest pencil in the world and look up at it and you'll realise how insignificant you are.

John's Explanatory Note: Don't stay there for too long though, or you'll start to lose all your self-confidence, and that could be dangerous if you've an arduous drive home from the Lakes through mountainous terrain and winding roads, etc.

After visiting the museum, Mary and I were in the tearoom and it was lovely and quiet – just the gentle murmur of chat and chink of teaspoons against china – when this big party of ten came in, and it had been raining so they all had cagoules on. They took them off in unison, and honestly, the cacophony of them doing that was sickening. (Plus, there was a lot of nose blowing going on.) It put me right off my blueberry muffin, though interestingly, Mary was absolutely fine and carried on eating her tiffin. Totally unaffected!

Duffel danger!

Oof, I've just seen a small man shuffling by in a duffel coat. I'm not so sure about duffel coats, not just because they have lots of toggles that could be misconstrued for annoying flies or jaspers, but because I've always thought seeing duffel coats can make people worry there's a nuclear bomb march in the vicinity, do you know what I mean? I don't mind toddlers sporting them or even that Paddington Bear, but this bloke, whoever he is, would have done better to pop a cagoule over a fleece and put the hood up. It would have afforded him the same protection without frightening people that there's going to be a nuclear war starting any moment.

––––––––––

John's Explanatory Note: If you do feel compelled to wear a duffel coat, you may find the hood flops over your head too much, impairing visibility and making walking difficult. This dilemma can be simply sorted by shoving a rolled-up scarf behind your neck, thereby forcing back the hood and restoring visibility. The only problem is you will now have an unsightly hump at the top of your back, and people will give you an even wider berth than duffel-coat wearers normally experience.

––––––––––

Oof, the funny little man in the duffel coat has doubled back and is approaching me. His hood is riding high, suggesting he's employing my suggestion and has a rolled-up scarf stuffed in there, but I didn't see an unsightly hump when he had his back to me. Hmm, he looks strangely familiar...

"Afternoon, John!" says Ken Worthington, his red face now clearly visible beneath the hood of his duffel coat.

"Aha, it's you, Ken!" I reply, pleased to see my next-door neighbour and sole agent, and keen to put our recent misunderstanding behind us. "Good to see you again, and I now understand why your duffel-coat hood isn't obscuring your eyes!"

"I beg your pardon?" says Ken, looking a bit confused.

"You don't have a rolled-up scarf behind your neck, do you?" I note to Ken, who has gone very red by now. "It's your Afro, isn't it — that's what's stopping the hood from flopping down onto your head, and allowing you to walk around freely with unimpaired vision?"

"I don't know WHAT you're on about!" replies Ken, irritably. "I was on my way to the shops when I spotted you talking to yourself. I thought I'd come and say hello and tell the readers the story of my recent shopping trip to Aldi, when I was traumatised by the beeping noises. I wasn't in the mood before, but I'm ready to tell it now."

"Oof, Ken," I reply, reproachfully. "You're way, way too late! That story has been relayed in its entirety by yours truly. We've discussed all the shopping dilemmas and we've moved on. The shopping chapter's over!"

"Ooh," says Ken, looking crestfallen. "It would have been better for the readers to hear the story from MY mouth, don't you think, John?"

"No, I don't, Ken!" I assure Ken, in quite a tough tone because he needs to realise we can't backtrack like this. "Besides, the story and its reference to electronic baby birds is a little odd for a family publication like this, so I'm probably going to chop it out anyway. Far better, Ken, for you to explain to the readers why exactly you didn't want to get rid of your mildewy garden chairs and accept my gift of a bench with knockdown construction!"

"Mildewy chairs?" says Ken, his eyes narrowing. "That wasn't mildew – it was green crayon, scribbled on the chairs by my nephew Nathan when he was little."

"I find that extremely hard to believe, Ken," I say, wearily – Ken has given this ridiculous explanation so many times before, as the reason he wouldn't accept my fabulous gift of a garden bench for his 55th birthday a few years ago.

"But it's true!" hisses Ken, angrily, his duffel-coat hood flopping forwards a bit, but then the natural springiness of his Afro forcing it back to its former position. "And if you say any different, when I come to proofread this book, I'll simply strike out the offending words. And in their place I'll insert the true tale of my traumatic trip to Aldi – IN MY OWN WORDS!"

"Oof, Ken! You've overstepped the mark!" I say, aghast. "That's interfering with an artist's work."

"No, it isn't – it's making the artist tell the truth!" says Ken, tossing his head back furiously, but his hood is trapped on his Afro so it doesn't slide off his head as you might expect. Ken looks around a bit before sitting down on the bench next to me and letting out a long sigh.

"Can I be frank with you, John?" he says, finally.

"I'd like you to be, yes please, Ken." I reply, eagerly.

"This book of yours. I'm sorry to say, will have a very limited appeal…"

"How do you know that?" I ask, taken aback slightly by Ken's bluntness.

"…UNLESS!" Ken suddenly strikes up, "you can see your way into, erm… spicing it up a little!"

"I'm sorry?" I answer, perplexed. Does Ken mean 'mention his curry takeaways'? If so, he can relax because I have done, but I'm not sure he DOES mean that.

"People nowadays want to read a bonkbuster, John," advises Ken, his beady eyes narrowing further. "You've got to spill the beans on your private life with Mary. That's how I'm going to be able to sell this in Asda and, erm… Costcutter – be nice to get a few copies in there.

"And the library, Ken?" I suggest, remembering that libraries do stock books still, although to be honest most people prefer to browse the DVD section or go on the computers, don't they?

"Hmm, I suppose so," says Ken, without enthusiasm. "What's the title of this epic then?"

"*Two Margarines and Other Domestic Dilemmas*," I reply, proudly. Ken squints into the distance. He appears to be thinking.

"How about: *Patio Positions: Confessions of a Suburban Husband*!" Ken suggests, before adding with a wicked grin, "Or: *Net Curtains: The Real Reason They're Twitching*!"

I consider Ken's suggestions carefully before taking a deep breath and replying, "Well, Ken. These are all great ideas, but those subjects are already comprehensively being dealt with. There's a whole section devoted to curtain care, and we'll be discussing patios and barbecue furniture in a later chapter, provisionally titled: 'Relax Before Teatime'."

"Grrr… you just don't get it, do you!" growls Ken, before leaping up off the bench, and swinging his string shopping bag over his shoulder. "Well, please yerself! I'm off to the delicatessen to buy some stuffed olives steeped in brine!"

"Oof, is that wise, Ken?" I say, in a genuinely caring tone, because I'm not sure it IS wise buying things like that.

Ooh, Ken hasn't replied. He's walking off in a huff. What a strange man he is – his Cuban heels clicking angrily on the library forecourt paving slabs, and his duffel-coat hood flapping. (His Afro is no longer trapping the hood, by the way. Perhaps it's time for a scarf to be inserted to make the hood tighter?) But I'm glad Ken's going because he was becoming rather annoying, I think you'll agree, readers. And yet we should be grateful to Ken because without realising it, he's reminded me of the final section of this chapter.

Why do some shops still have their doors shut during opening hours? It's crazy, isn't it?

It certainly is, and our local delicatessen is a prime offender. To go inside you have to laboriously open the door before you can walk in! Not that I'd go in there anyway, cos everything in that shop looks a bit funny to me. It only sells stuff no one in their right minds would consider buying, like olives, and strange herbs in glass jars. No Cup-a-Soups, or Pot Noodles, or sensible items like that. You could argue then that everything in that shop should be free. But it isn't – it's extremely pricey, and to cap it all, they have a door with an old bell that rings when the door opens and shuts. Non-electronic – very unfashionable.

Shoppers prefer doors to be wedged open nowadays, don't they, so entry and exit is swift and trouble-free? Plus the advantage is, the heat rushes out of the shops and warms up shoppers as they trudge along the cold streets during the long winter months. Yes, I realise it makes the shops very cold inside, but that can lead to witty exchanges between customer and shop assistant. "Ooh, it's freezing out there today!" says the shopper, parking their trolley. "Yes, and it's even colder in here!" replies the assistant, blowing on their fingers. Surely the community coming together in this way through a shared experience outweighs the risk of increased global warming? It doesn't? Oh all right then. It's just that you can't deny – a freezing shop can only help boost sales of fleeces, and body warmers!

The fabulous 'post office' body warmer revolution

Have you been in your local post office recently? I notice they've started wedging their doors open, well, our local post office has, although for years they resisted. But now it's so cold inside there during the winter that the assistants have all been issued with eye-catching body warmers displaying the post office logo. Fantastic! They wear them all day long now as they serve, and it's a super development in the marvellous history of the post office. Hats off to them – I mean, hats on, it's so blinkin' cold!

Well, Mary's just texted me to say that she and Joan have bumped into her friend Doreen Melody in the pound shop and the three ladies are now going to Peacock's to hunt for some new tights for Joan, so I'm to see Mary back at the house. I'm a bit disappointed not to be driving home with Mary, but obviously I can't join the ladies on such a sensitive shopping mission. So I shall walk back to the supermarket car park with the shopping before loading my Austin Ambassador and driving home in readiness for the next domestic activity and its attendant dilemmas: cooking our dinner (or 'lunch', as posh people call it).

Shame I'm driving back, in a way. If I was on foot I might see an elastic band on the pavement. Or several elastic bands. Once I picked up seven while walking our dog, Kirsty. Or I might spy a lost glove on a wall. Aha! I've written a song about this heart-breaking phenomenon, because you do see them abandoned on a wall or gatepost on your way back from the shops in winter time, don't you? This is a haunting ballad, readers, with some long high notes requiring good lung capacity and expert breath control. Barbara Dickson would have a field day with this one. Alternatively, it could be a crowd-pleasing anthem for an emerging personality vocalist like Liam Gallagher, although I'd prefer it if he didn't keep his hands behind his back. Yes, normally that's good manners, but while singing this song he'll need to have them stretched out in front of him, imagining he's reaching for the poor little glove.

GLOVE ON THE WALL

Glove on a wall
Rain-sodden and small
Some little child
Must have let it fall

Poor little mite
One hand warm, one with frostbite
Though my thoughts are all
With the glove on the wall

Look at this glove, once it was loved
Now it lies dirty and frozen
Maybe the glove had had enough
Of being a pair and felt chosen

To go it alone
And live on a stone
If so, now I bet
It's filled with regret
Missing its mate
Who now shares its fate
For no one can love
A solitary glove

Glove on the wall
You're just like us all
Lonely, but too proud
To say it out loud

Glove on the wall
I'll answer your call
Find you a hand to hold
A mitten I once found in the road
It's warm in my holdall
Glove on the wall!

CHAPTER 11:

UNACCOMPANIED LADY
(THE ART OF LETTUCE SPINNING)

You can't have your dinner until you've spun the lettuce – if you're having lettuce for your dinner, which we are today. (Not just lettuce, don't be daft – we're not on a health farm, you know!) As I speak, Mary is warming through a cheese flan in the side oven. She could have microwaved it, yes, but we want the crust to be nice and crusty, and essentially live up to its name, I suppose is what I'm saying. Alongside the flan will be consumed some new potatoes, low-fat coleslaw, sliced beetroot (crinkle cut), other assorted pickles including piccalilli, and a side salad. And this is why I'm currently in the garden holding a lettuce spinner, which I'm about to spin very, very quickly.

I'm using a 'cage' lettuce spinner, not a 'cog-driven' salad spinner where you turn a handle, which is designed for interior use with the operator sat hunched over the spinner. Yes, we have one of those and Mary likes to use it, but frankly, I don't. It makes me feel like I'm an impoverished weaver from the olden days. If I was sporting a collarless shirt, waistcoat and hobnailed boots with a flat cap and even a neckerchief then yes, maybe it would feel right, but then again it would feel horribly wrong because I'd be dressed like a folk singer, and oof, I'm sorry to tell you this, readers, but I don't like folk music. Not just because they cup their ear with their hand and suddenly bang their foot down hard, startling everyone. (Whose idea was it to start doing that? It's ridiculous!) No, it's because I believe folk music encourages slovenly dress, I really do.

———————

John's Explanatory Note: I don't like jazz music either, because there's too many notes and they never seem to be in the right order, have you noticed? It seems crazy that they can continue to be allowed to get away with it!

———————

Can folk music ever be enjoyable?

I can't believe I'm saying this but... yes, on extremely rare occasions it can. Last autumn, Mary and I were searching for a shopping channel on the TV so Mary could check out the foot spa they were demonstrating, when we accidentally came across an obscure Celtic music channel. There was a folk band playing with a heavy rock guitarist and there was a piper in a kilt. I think they must have employed a wind machine as his kilt was fluttering quite a bit, and the camera was swooping over the audience, which seemed to comprise ordinary members of the public like me and Mary – you know, not too many men in waistcoats with long hair and beards – which was pleasing to witness. No, the ladies were in nice floral tops and the gentlemen were sporting leisure shirts.

I even saw one chap with a cream pullover draped over his shoulders, which was a lovely sight, and a look I've admired ever since I saw actor John Nettles wearing one in an episode of popular TV series *Bergerac*.

So we watched this folk band and the kilt fluttering for a while and Mary began nodding approvingly, and I have to say they weren't half bad. In fact, they were excellent, and I began tapping my toe. Then I suggested to Mary that we should copy the TV audience and start clapping along, but she said she was all right just listening. I would have clapped on my own, but I had the remote in my hands and I'd have had to put it down, and anyway after a while Mary said, "Where's this foot spa you're showing me then, John?" so I flicked over onto the shopping channel, but it was a set of necklaces by then which looked a bit pricey. When we switched back to the music channel, it was a big lad in a tight shirt walking through a field doing opera singing, but he was no Sir Harry Secombe so we turned over to UK Gold and watched *Taggart*.

Anyway, that band stuck in my mind. I thought – considering it was folk music it wasn't half bad, and I suggested to Ken Worthington he should sign them to his rostrum, but he couldn't find their contact details, so he claims. We'd watched them in Ken's office on his computer, on – you know – Youbend, but I think Ken was frightened by the piper with the fluttering kilt, who also had long hair that was tied in a knot at the top of his head, which our Karen claims is called a 'man bun'. Is that right? I haven't heard that before and I wasn't sure if she was having me on or not...

This pic from yesteryear needs no explanation — except to say at the time I was a big Roger Whittaker fan, and sported a slight quiff. I'm still a fan of Roger's — but the quiff has long gone!

Mary's dreadful blunder

Oof, perhaps I shouldn't have put that subtitle as Mary won't be happy when she reads it. But, to be honest, readers, will she ever read it? I mean, YOU'RE bothering to read this book and I'm very grateful to you for doing so (and it's why I'm calling you 'readers'), but, let's face it — most people don't have time to read books any more and Mary's exactly the same. She reads her texts and her Facebook messages, and the instructions on the label of the surface spray but she has little time to read anything else. Any downtime Mary does have she'll spend catching up on the TV soaps, or on the phone to our Karen because she's living in Mansfield now with her friend Maxine. I didn't tell you that, did I? Why would I? It's personal info.

But go on then – since I've started divulging personal information, I'll continue. Karen's known Maxine since girlhood, and they now rent a flat together, in Mansfield, as I've already stated. Maxine's a palliative nurse, and Karen is a nursery assistant at a nursery called Tiny Feet, although here's a thing – one child who attends has size 5 feet, which is enormous for a 4-year-old, isn't it? Bigger than Mary's, which come in at 3½, size 4 for Wellington boots, although she doesn't wear things like that any more. Well, does anybody? They're something from the past, aren't they, Wellington boots, when people used to walk more in puddles? But as a nation we've seen sense and we avoid that kind of thing now if we can, don't you think? We drive everywhere, which is lovely, or we get a minicab for six or seven pounds – fantastic!

I must just say, with some sadness, that Mary doesn't even seem to have time to listen to my new songs these days. I used to play her all my new ones and she'd give me a critique, which was usually like Ken's – "Mm, needs a bit more work, that one, John" – but now she's always too busy to even listen, never mind comment, which is a shame.

Having said that, recently I was playing my organ in the lounge, and I looked up and caught Mary with her eyes shut and an ear cocked to one side, and I thought, "Oh, she must be listening to me." I was performing a new song (later abandoned) called 'Wanna Crack A Nut With Me?', a calypso-based ditty all about inviting someone to sit and pick up the nut crackers and have a go, because it's not that easy, is it?

John's Explanatory Note: Sometimes the nuts fly out of the crackers and across the room, which although it causes great hilarity, it's not that funny if you don't get your nut in the end, is it? Perhaps you're best off sharing a packet of peanuts?

Anyway, then I remembered that Mary had strained her neck at step class earlier that evening, and sure enough, she proceeded to move her head the other way and then back again, with a slight grimace on her face. So that's what it was. She wasn't listening to me at all – she was exercising her poorly neck! Ooh yes, she does step class as well, and spinning class (not the medieval craft where she'd have to wear a bonnet, that would be akin to liking folk music, no, I mean the type of spinning where you cycle very quickly): two more examples of how busy Mary is these days and why I don't think she'll have time to read that subtitle about making a dreadful blunder, which I haven't even mentioned yet, but I'm going to right now!

A few summers ago in a moment of utter madness, Mary Shuttleworth gave away our old lettuce spinner to the charity shop without even consulting me first! As soon as I found out I rushed round to the charity shop and they told me – wait for it – not that they'd sold it, but that they'd thrown it away as they didn't think anyone would have bought it. (That was a dreadful blunder as well!) You see, I would have bought it, and I was hopping mad with Sheila for doing that. She's been volunteering there fourteen years and should have known better. As should Mary, who just shrugged when challenged about the incident – she didn't apologise properly, in my view.

Luckily (for you, readers, obviously, but for me in particular), the story doesn't end there. The following week I was driving near the village of Penistone, after returning a faulty audio cable to an electrical store in the vicinity, when I pulled the car over to talk to a horse grazing in a field. There on the ground next to the bottom of the dry-stone wall I spotted a lettuce spinner! Not the one Mary chucked – that would have been too incredible. Another lettuce spinner, and in a very sorry state, all covered in moss. I popped it in the boot of my Ambassador and took it back to our house, after I'd had a little chat with the horse – not easy as it was grazing at the far end of the field. When I got home I scraped the moss and other associated debris off the lettuce spinner before soaking it in disinfectant and soapy water and scrubbing it thoroughly with a brush. Once I'd dried it and buffed it up nicely with a lint-free cloth, I showed it to Mary, who inspected it, before (grudgingly) approving it as a kitchen utensil to be employed on an everyday basis, although it's only me that ever uses it.

Come on then − spin the blinkin' lettuce!

Yes, I'm about to, please be patient. Um, I've just remembered that Karen's flatmate, Maxine, is quite good on the acoustic guitar. She can do fingerpicking like Mary Hopkin, the fabulous welsh songstress, and that's a skill I've always admired. I tried doing it once because Maxine used to leave her guitar on Karen's floor cushion for weeks on end, but it was too tricky. Mind you, as I always say − why learn fingerpicking when you can play all the same notes on an electronic organ employing acoustic guitar (instrument 42), and have a cracking rhumba drum beat playing as you do so?

Right, I'm standing on the patio, legs well apart to provide a solid anchor because the furious windmill action my arms will soon be doing could make me topple over if I'm not properly grounded. Just so you know what's coming: I shall whirl my extended arm round and round in the air while holding on to the spinner until all the moisture has left the lettuce and exited the cage − courtesy of centrifugal force − and the lettuce leaves inside have become crisp and dry. (I obviously don't mean until they turn into a bottle of vegetable oil, although some magicians could do that trick, I'm sure, with the right preparation!)

"John?" calls Mary from the back door. "Where's my blinking lettuce?"

"Oof, sorry love," I reply. "I got distracted. I'll be in with it very shortly!"

"Well, hurry UP! Everything's ready and the flan's getting cold!" Mary shouts crossly. "You should have used the proper salad spinner, not that rotten bit of plastic!"

"Oof, Mary!" I say, sounding a bit hurt, but Mary can't hear me as she's gone back inside, slamming the door behind her.

Right, as I spin the lettuce I'm going to sing a little ditty to spur myself on. Mary's departure is most opportune, as the lyric of this one tells the true story of the only occasion I've ever looked at another lady since I've been married. While some readers may find the story shocking, ALL readers will be shocked to learn that it's in the folk music idiom! I know – what am I playing at? I tried dearly to make it a country and western number, but it just came out as folk. So sing along, but please – no foot banging on key phrases!

UNACCOMPANIED LADY

I was at a conference for security personnel
They'd just completed the opening address when I started to feel
    unwell
So I picked up my factpack and tiptoed out to the Gents for a
    quick splashdown
Then I popped to the bar for an orange juice and I saw as I sat
    down

An unaccompanied lady sitting at the bar
Unaccompanied lady – I wonder who you are

Who she was was plain because she wore on her lapel
A badge which bore the name 'Denise' from the Derbyshire town
    of Bakewell
She was a beauty oh so rare, I trembled as I saw
Her stoop to retrieve a packet of nuts she'd dropped upon the floor

An unaccompanied lady sitting at the bar
Unaccompanied lady – I wonder who you are

At that moment a man appeared – her husband I presume
He kissed her and briskly whisked her away, back to the
   conference room
I saw them later in the carvery sharing a leg of lamb
And cursed myself for forgetting briefly that I'm a married man

Ooh, unaccompanied lady sitting at the bar
Unaccompanied Lady – I wonder where you are

"Ooh cheeky!" comes a familiar voice from behind one of the conifers that separates my property from the bungalow of you-know-who!

"Who's saying that?" I shout, stopping my lettuce spinning, although I know EXACTLY who it is.

"It's me – your proofreader! I'm delighted to hear you're turning your book into a saucy bonkbuster with salacious revelations!", says Ken Worthington, chuckling lasciviously as he appears in a gap between two miniature conifers.

"Hello Ken," I say, warily. "It was a very long time ago, and I do assure you AND the readers that nothing untoward occurred between myself and lady from Bakewell. Look, it's super to see you, Ken, but I've no time to engage in conversation right now. I'm spinning the lettuce for Mary and then I'm disappearing inside to eat my dinner."

"Well, I'm having mine right now!" replies Ken, proudly, as he raises his hands, revealing a bowlful of – ooh – I don't know what it is. It looks a bit funny to me.

"Is that really your lunch, Ken?" I ask, warily still (i.e. my mood hasn't changed in the last thirty seconds, since I was last wary).

"It certainly is!" replies Ken. "Salad with edamame beans, falafel and beansprouts."

"Oof, no, Ken," I say, slightly alarmed. (Yes, my mood has changed now, readers!) "You're likely to experience severe tummy trouble eating things like that."

"Don't be silly, John," argues Ken, shoving a forkful of the strange concoction into his mouth.

Luckily, I've just remembered the rest of the song 'Tummy Trouble' (I sang a snatch of it a while ago, remember?)

"Ken?" I suggest, excitedly. "Let me sing you verses two and three of my classic composition, 'Tummy Trouble'. You're advised – for medical reasons – to stop eating and to listen carefully to the lyrics."

"Ooh right, John, yes I will. Thank you!" replies Ken, and he puts his bowl down and sits on the low boundary wall to listen to my song as I trust you will too, readers!

TUMMY TROUBLE (VERSES 2 & 3)

Tummy trouble brings misery to your life
Tummy trouble provokes anger in your wife
For when you say your tummy hurts
She knows from past experience
Bad odours will be coming soon to the living room

"Lovely stuff, John!" chuckles Ken. "You've gone from extra marital disclosures to good old lavatorial humour. We're finally on your way to creating a best-seller. Next verse, please!

"Oof, I'm not sure what you mean, Ken," I reply, "but yes, here's the next verse!"

Tummy trouble – but please don't be alarmed
Tummy trouble – your tummy can be calmed

Milk of Magnesia
Tends to make things easier
Relief for many comes with a Rennie.

"Relief for MANY comes with a RENNIE!" repeats Ken exuberantly as he gets up and clambers onto the low boundary wall.

"Oof, no, Kenneth!" I say, breaking off from singing to observe Ken's tomfoolery.

"Tummy trouble! I've got tummy trouble!" Ken wails while attempting to dance on the wall AND eat from his weird lunch bowl AT THE SAME TIME!

"Ken, what on earth are you doing?" I enquire anxiously. "Your Cuban heels are threatening the fabric of the wall, and you're going to damage it if you don't dismount. Dismount immediately!"

"Ooh ducky!" says Ken, chuckling devilishly.

"Please get off the wall, Ken!"

"No, I won't!"

"Very well," I say with a sigh. "You leave me no option but to reactivate the lettuce spinner!"

Yep readers, I'm whirring my arm now and aiming the water droplets that are flying from the spinner towards Ken and they're catching his Afro full on. He no longer has his duffel coat on so without its hood his Afro has no protection from the spray. In fact, he's wearing a Hawaiian shirt and Bermuda shorts so he's extremely vulnerable. Ha ha! It's catching Ken full on, and he's putting his arm up to protect his face and as a result his weird salady meal has toppled from his grasp and onto the ground where it belongs!

"You flipping idiot!" shouts Ken, angrily – but secretly he must realise I've done him a favour by saving him from eating that, which would surely have given him a very poorly tummy.

"Mary's right, John, you are behaving very strangely today," whimpers Ken as he shakes water droplets from his hair, trying to scoop up the remnants of his meal from off our patio back into his bowl. I hope he's not planning to eat that or it WILL give him a poorly tummy!

"You're alienating your friends now," continues Ken, peevishly, "as well as your family!"

Oof, Mary's appeared and she doesn't seem very happy.

"John! I saw what you did to Ken. You silly, silly man!" says Mary, with a face of thunder. "Ken, come to our house and I'll get you a towel."

"I'm sorry, Mary," I say, then turning hopefully to Mary, I add, "but you'll be pleased to learn that the lettuce is now as dry as a bone!"

But Mary is ignoring me, and Ken is too, and they both march in through the back door of our house, leaving me outside with the salad spinner. Oof, perhaps I was a bit hard on Ken, but he didn't heed my warnings, so drastic measures needed to be taken.

I'm disappointed in Mary. Despite being a dinner lady she hasn't given me any domestic dilemmas to consider, and is highly unlikely to. The only thing she said recently that I might be able to use for this book was when she was baking and she started giving me some advice on 'How to assemble a crumble', but I didn't take in a word she said. All I could think was 'assembling a crumble' is a contradiction in terms. It's not possible surely – to assemble something that's crumbling away in yer hand! It's like 'knockdown construction', which was written on the bench instructions at the hardware shop, the one I tried to buy for Ken. I asked to speak to the manageress because 'knockdown construction' is clearly a contradiction in terms. How can you construct something if you're knocking it down? Of course, she had no answer...

I have to tell you, readers, my arm hurts from all this lettuce spinning, and my head hurts from trying to write a book in a day.

I'd much rather be sat in my garage now playing my organ. I was banned from the lounge, you see, because my organ interfered with the TV. Even when I was wearing headphones there would be spillage, and Mary claims my breathing became erratic and raspy. Obviously, I couldn't hear because I had my headphones on. So I was moved to the garage with the organ placed on top of our chest freezer. My seat is a twenty-four pack of Diet Sprite, which obviously gets lower as the cans are transferred to the house for public consumption. But I don't mind – I welcome the challenge of reaching ever higher. In winter it gets a bit cold in the garage, even with my fleece on, so I tend to play in the bedroom with the organ on the bed. But then I get disturbed by Mary coming in with clean laundry, and it puts me off my stride.

I should have my own song-writing room really, with a keyboard stand and a nice leather stool, and a sign on the door saying 'Do not disturb!' Sammi Martini (another of Ken's acts) has a set-up like that, and his mum's not allowed to disturb him while he's compiling his tapes. Mind you, they're not tapes any more, his backing tracks are all on his laptop, apparently, and according to Ken he's developed a very shrewd onstage technique. While Sammi's singing the final chorus of the current song, and everyone's clapping along, he strides over to his laptop and searches for the next song (dancing on the spot all the while) so that the next song's all lined up. So then all Sammi has to do is press a button, once he's finished the song that he's still singing. Seamless, and extremely clever, in my view.

Sammi's just had a new publicity card printed. It says on it that he's got a 'quicksilver wit'. The thing is, Sammi works for Kwikfit in the daytime, so I don't know why he hasn't put 'Kwiksilver wit'. Maybe his wit isn't that quick after all, or 'Kwik' even! Still, he's doing very well. So is Janet Le Roe, who's got a guitar with a sheep on it. (Not a real sheep, obviously, that would be too heavy to carry – it's a sticker of a sheep.) Janet accompanies a storyteller called Val – I don't know her second name, sorry, I can't help you there – at a carvery every Sunday not too far from the Abbeydale Industrial Hamlet. Fantastic! The storyteller... ooh, it might be Cooper... Val Cooper, but don't hold me to it, erm... has a staff which she bangs hard if there's too much chatter from the kids, and then Janet has to do some gentle fingerpicking till they've settled. Yes, her and Sammi are doing very, very well. Better than me... THEY get paid when they do their engagements, you know. THEY don't just get their petrol money, like I do.

I'll end the chapter, if I may, with the final verse of 'Tummy Trouble', which I wasn't able to sing due to Ken's errant behaviour. I won't spin as I sing. I think this lettuce has been spun enough!

And when you're feeling better
And you're tucking into a Viennetta
You'll feel well enough to post a letter
Or walk a red setter!

(*But don't let them off the lead, is my advice, as they're daft as a brush, that breed, and very fleet of foot if they run away, and if they do that you're going to get very anxious trying to catch them. And with anxiety comes more...*)

Tummy trouble!
Ho ho ho – tummy trouble!

Right, well, I'd better go inside now and present this lettuce to Mary. Wish me luck, and (hopefully) I'll see you on the next page!

CHAPTER 12:

DINING DILEMMAS
(HAVE YOU SEEN MY WIFE? PART 2)

I expected to come into the kitchen and find Ken perched on my bar stool, with a towel draped around his shoulders, tucking into my flan, but the truth is far worse! Mary and Ken have quit the premises, and I'm wondering if they might have been kidnapped, because Mary's bag is still here with her brand new sweeteners in it. Mary would never have left home without her bag except in a hostage-taking situation. I'm hoping that my fears are unwarranted, and yet, without wishing to appear rude, right now I'd be quite pleased if I found out Ken had been kidnapped because he damaged the low boundary wall. A short period bound and gagged in the back of a van might give Ken time to reflect on his foolish actions and decide to apologise to me and generally become a better person.

John's Explanatory Note: If my attitude towards Ken seems a little harsh, let me inform you that after a close inspection of the wall, a small section of mortar between two coping stones was discovered to be chipped, consistent with a Cuban heel violently striking it, and a deposit of strange noodly stuff from Ken's meal was found upon the wall, which will need removing with rubber gloves and the ground power-washing, so no – Ken is not my favourite person at the moment!

Another possible scenario is that Mary and Ken went round to Ken's for their dinner. The flan is missing (or is that further evidence of kidnappers? They'd surely want something to munch as they career down country lanes in their van, laughing nastily as they reflect on their wicked deed). Or perhaps Mary has just hidden the flan, and Ken has driven Mary to the garden centre in his Honda Civic for a 2 for 1 special lunch to get back at me for spraying him with water droplets. Whatever has happened, they're both behaving very selfishly, and not having Mary sitting at the family table eating lunch with me now completely ruins the flow of my book, which is supposed to be dealing with family dining dilemmas. Instead we'll have to jump straight to this section:

The perils of eating alone

When you're eating alone, it's very difficult to know where to look, isn't it, as you're munching? Your eyes are going all over the shop, and while it's not a bad idea to occasionally check the ceiling of the room you're eating in to ascertain there are no loose lumps of plaster about to fall on your head, it can put a strain on your neck, and food could become lodged in your windpipe. And because you're alone there's going to be no one to pat you on the back as you cough and splutter, or – in extreme cases – perform artificial respiration on your lifeless body. At this early stage in discussing the dilemma I really must digress to consider:

The curious case of Julie Satan and the night she nearly killed Ken!

Julie Satan is Ken's main speciality act. Leeds-based, Julie sports a leopardskin basque and wields a broadsword (donated by her boyfriend, Mick, who collects military memorabilia, apparently) as she mimes to heavy rock classics. During guitar solos Julie bends her knees and flicks her tongue in and out like a poisonous snake, which is quite clever, in my view. She had green hair for a while, which would shock some people, but after a while you accepted it. Julie, incidentally, used to work for Williams and Glyn's bank but that was a heck of a long time ago – William and Glyn sold their business in the early eighties, as I recall. I've not the faintest what they did then, but Julie went to work for the council organising trips to the swimming baths for naughty children.

Anyhow, one particular evening, Ken went to visit Julie at an undisclosed address in Sowerby Bridge near Halifax (I can't disclose the address because I simply don't know it!), where the wine flowed and showbiz banter ensued, and at one point Ken told a slightly saucy joke. Julie – so Ken alleges – then said "Ooh, get you!", and did that thing with her hand like Bet Lynch off *Coronation Street* used to do. You know, she bent her wrist and her hand flopped forward and her long fingernails caught Ken on his windpipe and he started choking uncontrollably. But Julie thought he was laughing, and she said, "Ooh Ken, you shouldn't be laughing at your own joke!" (which of course you shouldn't). But Ken wasn't laughing – he was fighting for his life!

How did we get on to that? Oh, I know – my point is Ken might have died if he'd been alone, but luckily he didn't die because Julie was able to thump his back really hard and then perform some abdominal thrusts upon Ken (the 'Heinlich Manoeuvre', I believe it's called), grabbing him round his chest from behind and yanking until his breathing had returned to normal. And I've a message for Julie if she's reading this: hello Julie – I trust you're well, and thank you for saving Ken's life. I'm proud to call you a stablemate... though may I suggest you trim your fingernails!

So where should you look while eating alone?

You could read a book, I suppose, but that seems a bit rude while you're eating, and you might accidentally smear some cottage cheese on a page, but that would serve you right for reading at the table, and for eating cottage cheese, an' all. It's unpleasant stuff, in my view, yet I've seen Mary and Joan Chitty piling it onto Ryvitas like there's no tomorrow.

John's Explanatory Note: I'm glad to say Mary doesn't eat humus – although a lot of folk love it, don't they? I don't know why because it derives from compost, doesn't it? They dip a carrot baton into it, and ooh no, I don't advise doing that, it's dirty! I went to a funeral recently and they had humus in little dishes and I couldn't believe it – it seemed a bit disrespectful. Quiche and vol-au-vents and some triangular sandwiches on white bread only – that's what you need at a funeral. Ooh, I can feel a song coming on, but first let me finish this very important section.

In recent years the problem of where the solo diner should focus their attention while chewing their dinner has been eradicated by the arrival of the smartphone, which the user can just stare at like a zombie. But what if the battery's flat? Well, you could watch the phone charging up, I suppose, but you might as well watch paint dry (it's a lot more interesting than people realise, you should try it some time!). But hey, there's a better solution…

The ideal focus for solo diners

I'm perched on our bar stool now in the kitchen having a cheese sandwich (with lettuce too, naturally, although it's a bit dry and slightly bruised from being spun so much). Just a few inches from my face is our notice board. Interestingly enough, there are no notices on it, but there's something better: a minicab card. My son Darren picked it up a few years ago, after he'd enjoyed a night out with Plonker, and I thought it would be useful to pin it on the board in case Mary and I ever require transport to a wedding reception in the area, or another type of private function to which we were invited. Sadly, the opportunity to use it hasn't cropped up yet, but it's fantastic to know we can call the number if ever we need to.

On the card is a nice drawing that bears repeated studying and gives excellent focus for the solo diner. It shows a man stood next to a car and he's dressed as a chauffeur looking quite proud. He has a peaked cap and he's holding open the door of the car that looks very posh, although Darren said it was just a Ford Focus he rode in, which surprised me given the quality of the vehicle hinted at in the drawing.

There are also shopping-offer coupons, of course, pinned on our notice board, and I suspect yours is no different. These can be studied as you eat alone and 'valid till' dates checked and verified. If any are discovered to be out of date, remove them immediately, taking care when you extract the drawing pin not to drop all the other coupons on the floor, and do remember there might be a postcard from a relative being held up by the same pin. Yeah, it's not so easy eating alone, is it? And it gets worse…

Have I got food on my face?

What happens if you deposit food on your face during consumption of a meal? If you're eating with a partner or friend they can and hopefully will point it out immediately and the residue will be wiped away swiftly and safely in a controlled environment. If you miss it on your first attempt, any caring fellow diner will help you locate its exact position, and let you know when you've successfully removed the offending bit of food. Eating alone you're simply not going to notice if a small piece of carrot lodges itself on your chin, or a blob of gravy is nestling on your upper lip. Once, after I'd enjoyed a bowl of celery soup, there was a tiny strand of celery stuck in my teeth. Mary noticed that as I was talking it was flapping about a bit. She was able to alert me to this and I removed the celery strand under her supervision, but had I been dining alone it could have remained there flapping away all day long!

How do I know it's food on the face and not a growth?

This dilemma does pop up now and then, although, thankfully, it's rare. My advice is this: if you think someone has food on their face but you don't know their face very well, for example a stranger that's sitting on the next table in the garden centre cafe, don't point out a slice of beetroot on their ear because it might not be that at all – it might be a growth. To point that out would be extremely embarrassing for both parties, so exercise caution. In fact, maybe just keep your mouth closed, and say nothing (which you should do anyway if you're eating!).

How do I know it's a growth on the face and not food?

Interesting question, and not as daft as it sounds! As my wife of many years, Mary knows my face intimately, so has no hesitation in pointing out food deposits on it during a meal, and I'm heartily grateful to her for that. But on one particular occasion, she obviously hadn't been studying my face enough that day or she wouldn't have made the following grave error.

"John?" she said, pointing to my eye. "You've got a stye on your eyelid."

Now, I'd just finished eating a large portion of Mary's superb shepherd's pie (more of that later), so I was in a jubilant mood, but this sudden scary revelation killed that mood stone dead.

"I can't have, Mary!" I replied, incredulously.

It took a while to locate the exact location of the stye, and I grasped it very gingerly, in case it was painful. But I didn't feel a thing. In fact, the stye seemed to disintegrate to the touch, and as I looked at the finger that had touched the new growth, I noticed that it had a tiny blob of mashed potato on the end of it. So, that's what it was – it wasn't a stye, it was a blob of blinking mashed potato that must have been flicked from my over-enthusiastic fork onto my eyelid, but I was too engrossed in eating the shepherd's pie to notice. We both had a good chuckle about that, and it just goes to show that Mary isn't always right about what's on my face at meal times. But usually she is, and it's a shame that she's not here because if she was she'd be able to tell me if I've got any shards of crisps on my lips. (Yes, I've just had a packet of crisps with my sandwich, which I didn't tell you about, I realise, but then – I can't tell you everything!)

The man who appeared to be staring at me, but wasn't!

Once I was having a cup of tea and a piece of cake at the garden centre, taking advantage of the 'tea and cake deal', which operates from 2 till 4 each weekday afternoon. Although alone, I was fully occupied admiring the condiments receptacle, a cylindrical aluminium container with lots of perforations in it (presumably they're there to allow a good airflow around the salt and pepper pots, preventing any damp – and eventually mildew – from forming on them). Occasionally, I'd look up from the condiments receptacle and notice this old bloke sat on his own nearby eating a pork dinner (£5.95 and available all day!), but his eyes were all over the place as he ate. I felt quite sorry for him that he couldn't find anything to concentrate on while he was eating.

When I next looked up from the condiments receptacle – I'd got fed up of counting the holes, although my guesstimate is 325 – I saw that this bloke was looking directly at me, with a fixed unwavering stare. It seemed like he was trying to remember who I was and although I didn't recognise him, I realised he might know me from the drop-in centre, or his wife might have been a resident at one of the hospices I perform at. If so, he could have seen me one time when he was dropping off a bag of clothes or a dressing gown for her, if she was in the residents' lounge and I was in there playing on my organ. I've no idea but that could have been it. Anyway, if I knew him I'd forgotten who he was, but not wishing to be rude I nodded to him in a friendly manner. He seemed to be sort of nodding back, but continually, little nodding motions and this fixed stare. And then I realised he wasn't really looking at me – just concentrating hard on removing something from his mouth by probing repeatedly with his tongue.

John's Explanatory Note: Not like Julie Satan, of course, whose tongue movements on stage involve a rapidly repetitive flicking action. This chap's tongue movements were more minimal, and – thank goodness – occurring behind closed lips!

All became clear seconds later when his fingers went into his mouth and he pulled out a sizeable chunk of pork gristle, which I'm guessing must have got caught in his dentures, or maybe he had a cavity it had got lodged in. He deposited the offending food scrap on the side of his plate and carried on eating his meal, blinking a lot. But he'd stopped looking at me and now as he munched his dinner his eyes were all over the place again. Poor man – what a shame he wasn't close to a notice board!

Anyway, I can't really think of any more Dining Dilemmas, although I expect there's loads. Erm, should you wash your hands before you sit down at the table? Well, yes of course you should – that's not a dilemma – that's a given! If you're dining out the rules are more complex, but they're tackled in the next chapter.

Now, I mentioned quiche earlier and I really fancy a slice, because that sandwich and packet of crisps was insufficient. I'm hoping Mary will have saved me a slice of flan, which I'll be offered later as a peace offering when she returns, but will I accept it? We'll have to see. (It might have been gobbled up by the kidnappers, I realise, but that doesn't bear thinking about.) Of course, quiche is a bit posher than flan, and we rarely have it. In fact, it strikes me the only occasion you're guaranteed to find a nice slice of quiche is at a funeral tea. I think it would be fitting to end this rather sad and lonely chapter with a song which celebrates both quiche and the mysterious pleasure of...

MINGLING WITH MOURNERS

Thomas was a fine man
Lived to eighty-nine and
Eleven months he didn't quite
Make the big 'nine 0'
Though his life has ended
He's fondly remembered
Judging by the hordes
That to his wake did go.

Mingling with mourners
Some sat down in corners
Others by the table
Eyeing up the quiche
I've had days more jolly
But never lived more fully
Than when mingling with mourners
Remembering the deceased

Doris was an old girl
Who departed this world
When her invalid buggy
Tumbled off the kerb.
But Doris had a send-off
She would have been proud of
The trifle was excellent
The vol-au-vents superb!

Mingling with mourners
Some sat down in corners
Others by the table
Eyeing up the quiche
I've had days more jolly
But never lived more fully
Than when mingling with mourners
Remembering the deceased

Mingling with mourners
Some would say is creepy
Mingling with mourners
I disagree completely!

Mingling with mourners
Some would say is ghoulish
Mingling with mourners
I say "Don't be foolish!"

Bill had an allotment
Which to him – a lot meant
A Dutch hoe which got bent
His widow gave to me.
That Dutch hoe I'll cherish
I keep it in my garage
Though the head's so bent, it's rubbish
It couldn't hoe a single weed!

Mingling with mourners
Some sat down in corners
Others by the table
Eyeing up the quiche
I've had days more jolly
But never lived more fully
Than when mingling with mourners
Remembering the deceased…

So… enjoy the funerals you're lucky enough to attend while you can, folks! One day it will be your funeral and, although you will (strictly speaking) be in attendance, you won't be able to partake of the excellent fare including, I trust – a quality quiche. It's annoying, isn't it, but that's Life, I'm afraid. I mean – that's Death!

CHAPTER 13:

EATING OUT – THE EASY OPTION?

Just as there's often a quandary about whether to go out to a cafe for a coffee or stay at home with an instant, so – as you open your tin of baked beans (or baked beans with sausages, if it's a special occasion) for a quiet midday meal alone – the idea of dining out in a carvery with well-stocked salad bar looms large in your mind. Well, it does in mine, but often the prospect of having to check tyre pressures on my car, before consulting the AA website for conditions on the A621 to Baslow (not to mention changing out of my slippers into a stout outdoor shoe), makes me lose heart. And then if I notice a spot of rain on the lounge window, and Mary mischievously waves a packet of Ainsley Harriot soup in front of my face, I start to crumble and look for the TV remote. Am I getting old? Possibly, but home cooking's best, after all, in't it? Still, it can be a dilemma, deciding whether to dine in or out.

I realise some people (generally, students and other creatures of the night) are just getting out of bed as we're sitting down for our lunch, and I feel sorry for them, I really do. It must be awful to live your life so out of kilter. Those kinds of people are more likely to go for a meal at night-time, when it's dark and you should really carry a torch in your raincoat in case of a power cut, but I'm afraid this book doesn't cater for those sorts of people. And with a heavy heart I must admit this includes my next-door neighbour and sole agent, Ken Worthington.

Ken's nightly takeaway curry nightmare!

Oof, that subtitle might be a bit over the top. For all I know, Ken might enjoy going for a takeaway curry. He does it most nights so I suppose he must do. But he must be a masochist then – I wouldn't fancy it. Oof, no – for a start, he leaves his house before the end of *Pointless* (how can anyone do that?). We'll have had our tea and be all settled on the sofa for the evening, when we catch the top of Ken's Afro bobbing past the hedge as he heads to the Indian restaurant. It's a sorry sight indeed. Some nights Ken has been known to sit in and eat his curry at a table for one, but usually, as I've previously stated, he's too self-conscious to eat in – especially if there's courting couples or a large boisterous office group, perhaps celebrating somebody leaving?

John's Explanatory Note: Why do they do that, eh, celebrate someone leaving a job? It's publicly admitting that they're delighted they won't have to work with that person any more – SO pleased they're throwing a party to celebrate the fact! It's barmy, in my view, and the employee in question must be left feeling humiliated, a feeling offset only by all the lovely cards and leaving presents they receive... ooh, maybe the humiliation is worth it, after all!

If it's a takeaway Ken plumps for, he has to wait alone in a specially designated area for a good twenty minutes. Ken says he's allowed to read a newspaper that's lying there, help himself to complimentary Bombay mix from a little bowl, and even chat to the waiter at the bar, which all sounds lovely. However, the second the telephone rings with someone wanting to place an order or enquire about table availability, the waiter cuts Ken off stone dead, mid-conversation. It's like he doesn't exist any more to the waiter – awful!

Sometimes Ken whiles away the waiting time perched on a high bar stool (his short legs not reaching the chrome crossbar but left swinging helplessly) while sipping a Malibu (non-complimentary!), but the Bombay mix is now well out of Ken's range so that must be highly frustrating for him. When his takeaway finally arrives he has to carry it himself through the dark streets in a fragile paper bag, and the curry tends to leak out of the tray, weakening the bag still further. Once, while undertaking a routine check of the pointing in the wall outside our house, I spotted a tiny trail of brown deposits leading from the pavement up Ken's drive, which I'm convinced was a spill of curry from Ken's takeaway as he arrived back at his property. Ken strenuously denies this, but I'm sure I'm right. The next song is a cautionary tale aimed at Ken and all those who like to go out at night for a curry. Perhaps they would be better employed visiting an elderly relative…

HOW'S YER NAN?

It's night-time in the city
The streets begin to throb
With groups of lads and lasses
Heading to the pub
For some the evening ends alone
With a bag of chips
For others – an Indian meal with friends
Exchanging merry quips

But spare a thought for the OAP
Cowering behind their curtain
Too scared to go out at night
For fear of what may be lurking
As you munch your pompadoms
And twirl the pickle tray
Remember those who gave you life
And may need your help today

How's yer nan? How's yer nan?
Is more pressing a question than
Finding out about the state of an unleavened bread
That's what I said!
How's yer nan? How's yer nan?
Better find out while you can
Go and see her, before you hear she's dead!

Yes, why not pop round and see her
And while you do her chores
Enquire about her past
It might be more colourful than yours
You can help make old age a pleasure not a curse
So off you go... *(not right away, obviously)* – finish your curry first!

Oh, as you tuck in to your tarka dhal
She may have slipped and had a nasty fall
As you eat your beef madras
She may be breathing her last... gasp

How's yer nan? How's yer nan?
Is more pressing a question than
Finding out about the state of an unleavened bread
That's what I said!
How's yer nan? How's yer nan?
Better find out while you can
Go and see her, before you hear she's dead!

Look, I'm sure your nan is fine, but wouldn't it be a nice gesture just to check up on her (or him – it might be yer grandad!), instead of feeding your face in an Indian restaurant, or a Chinese one, or one of those posh brasseries with candles stuck in an old wine bottle (hmm, not so posh then – they saw you coming and hid the silver-plated candlesticks!). I've noticed that to gain admittance to these swanky places you often have to climb down rickety old steps into a basement. You may feel very sophisticated doing that but don't forget – come the end of the evening when you're full of food and the worse for wear through drink – you'll have to climb back up those steps!

The perils of dining out in a posh restaurant

The main one is obvious: however pleasant a meal in a posh restaurant is, you won't be able to enjoy it because you'll be so worried about the cost, if it's YOU paying the bill, that is! But if it hasn't yet been discussed who will be footing the bill and you'd rather not be the one doing that, then here's a clever way to get out of it:

> During the meal say to the person you're hoping will pay the bill, "Ooh, this is lovely – thank you for this!" Say it a few times (usually as you're starting to tuck in to each course), and if they don't seem to be getting the message, you can also throw in comments like: "This is so incredibly kind of you", and "My turn to treat YOU next time!", but use the last one very sparingly as it's not really very subtle, and of course it commits you to actually paying the next time you dine with that person!

What amazes me about posh restaurants is that often they don't have designated parking, so you can find yourself leaving your vehicle miles away from the restaurant and walking through busy streets looking for it. We had to do that a few years ago when we went to meet our Karen and her friend Maxine in a posh city centre restaurant to celebrate Karen gaining her NVQ Level 3 Diploma in Childcare, Learning and Development. Yes, you heard right!

A memorable meal with Mary and Maxine (and Karen!)

It was a nice summer's day and I was in a jovial mood, looking forward to celebrating with my wife, my daughter and her friend. I'd checked my car tyres and found them all to be at the correct level, which is always pleasing, isn't it? Mary had a nice summer dress on and I was sporting a cool (easy iron) short-sleeved shirt with a lightweight sweater draped over my shoulders (yep, just like Sergeant Bergerac!) in case it got chilly. Everything seemed hunky dory until we got to the restaurant and discovered there were double yellow lines everywhere, and so began a long journey to find somewhere to park. Finally, once parked, trying to locate the restaurant again became a nightmare. I was constantly looking up to check the name of the restaurant, which means you can't focus on which way you're walking, so I bumped into several people on the way, which made Mary angry, although I don't see why – I was the one who kept colliding and should have been cross!

When we finally entered the restaurant we had to stand in silence for ages waiting to be seated, and Mary pulled my sweater off my shoulders and made me hold it, but in doing so she had dislodged my shirt collar – you know, one side was riding up – but she wouldn't straighten it for me, so I wasn't happy about that. When we were finally greeted we were led straight to a table and made to sit down. I know that's normal practice in a posh restaurant but it's wrong, surely. The waiter should be showing you to the toilets so you can wash your hands (and then wait for you outside before showing you to the table? Yes, that would be nice but it's not essential).

But they never DO show you to the toilets to wash your hands, and that's dirty, in my view. So the dilemma is: should you and your fellow diners ignore the waiter when they ask you to follow them to the table, and instead all traipse off to the toilets so you can wash your hands? The answer is an emphatic 'Yes'! This may confuse the waiter, but it can't be helped. Hopefully, other diners would see what you were doing, get up from their table and follow you into the toilets. Wouldn't that be a smashing outcome? But it's a pipe dream. Until posh restaurants change their handwashing policy, you should perhaps avoid them and concentrate on the big three dining-out experiences...

Cafe, carvery or garden centre?

Dining out in an establishment without waiters is not only more hygienic – you also get to park your car nearby, you can sit down straight away (after washing your hands, please!) or, better still, you can queue up and receive a flag on a stick with a number on it (posh restaurants never think to give you one of them, do they?), and the experience will undoubtedly be kinder on your pocket. So the only real dilemma now is, which one should you choose?

The carvery

Carveries are nice, but access from the car park can be confusing and might be over uneven terrain. Also, is it me or are carveries getting bigger and bigger? They're often gigantic pubs nowadays on various levels, and finding your way around can be a nightmare. The music's gone a bit loud too, and young lasses in jeans seem to be replacing the mature ladies in aprons that I recall in the eighties who would lead you to the salad bar, and stress that you could help yourself to as much as you liked, but only as much as you could cram into a bowl during a single visit. I rose instantly to that challenge, wedging cucumber slices in around the bowl (as you would pieces of scrap wood to increase the capacity of your hired skip? Yes, absolutely, it's the same principle). But Mary wasn't happy with me doing that, so I wrote a song about it instead.

I know I said earlier that 'Life Is Like A Malibu Glass'. Well, I've changed my mind:

LIFE IS LIKE A SALAD BAR

In the restaurant of Life
Your table's chosen for you
Sometimes the wine is less than fine
And the other diners bore you
And throughout the night the waiter might
Totally ignore you
And if this metaphor has offended (I'm sorry, but...)
It's about to be extended!

Life is like a salad bar
You only get one visit
Take your bowl and follow me
I'll be your guiding spirit
Life is like a salad bar
Look too hard – you'll miss it
Life is like a salad bar... or is it?

Life is like a salad bar
As I've already stated
You're up there on your own
Excited and elated
Then all too soon you're back in your chair
Cursing and regretting
Oh, you got a lot, but you forgot
The thousand island dressing!

Live your life as I would
By your own nose be guided
But go easy on the onions
And use the tongs provided

Life is like a salad bar
You only get one visit
Take your bowl and follow me
I'll be your guiding spirit
Life is like a salad bar
Look too hard – you'll miss it
Life is like a salad bar… or is it?

———————————

John's Explanatory Note: I've heard that nowadays in some carveries you CAN go up and refill your salad bowl as many times as you like, so Life isn't really like a salad bar any more… unless you believe in reincarnation!

———————————

The cafe

What about popping out to the local cafe for a mixed grill, followed by cherry tart and custard? I used to do that when I was a younger man, before me and Mary were courting. But that's disappearing as an option too. You have to order something with a funny name like a panini or a charbatter (I believe that's how you spell it), and be confident in your pronunciation of 'mozzarella'. (Actually, it's quite easy, that one!) There'll be young professional people next to you tapping away on laptops, some with earphones talking to themselves. The menu is often chalked up on a board and indecipherable. Bowls of sugar on the table are becoming a

If in doubt dine at a Little Chef – its eye-catching menu the perfect focus for the solo diner. Someone needs to tell that lady behind me – her eyes are all over the place, look!

rarity. Instead you have to seek out a condiments station where all manner of sauces are to be found – if you can get to it! More often than not, someone will be standing in the way waiting for their speciality coffee to be made. And in order to procure it they have to divulge their name and have it written on the side of the cup for all to see! Isn't that a breach of data protection? It doesn't seem very well thought out, I must say, and makes me conclude that the safest place to go for your midday meal is…

The garden centre

The garden centre is the 'go to' venue for millions of normal law-abiding members of the public to get a nourishing meal at a reasonable price, allowing you to afford to buy a bag of compost on the way out. (The 3 for 2 deal generally applies, but please check as offer varies!) And if the cafe queue is long that day, or you're stressed for whatever reason (perhaps you couldn't find the napkins?), you can relax after you've dined by paying homage to the bronze Buddha statue. Except you can't because, infuriatingly, they've moved it from the water feature section to right by the entrance. So there you are, crouched upon your haunches, trying to connect spiritually with the bronze Buddha, but the automatic doors are opening and closing next to your head and people are trying to get around you with their trollies while you're trying to meditate. It's not ideal, is it?

So I've started boycotting the Buddha and instead I visit the squatting frog that's holding an upturned lily in its hand. Water comes out of the frog's mouth and lands in the lily – very clever, but there's a problem: the frog has a permanent smirk, like it knows it's clever, and that puts you against him. He needs to display more humility, like the milkmaid who carries a pail on each shoulder. It must be very heavy, but she doesn't seem unduly stressed by her ordeal. She's a plucky lass, there's no denying, so next time I visit the garden centre, I might go and spend some time with the milkmaid... but, oof, I might wait till Mary's looking at the geraniums!

The other negative of dining out at the garden centre is that, despite the recent expansion of the catering facilities and other wonderful sections, including patio furniture, barbecue accessories, kiddies' bedroom name-plates, etc., they still seem to be selling loads of plants and flowers, which, although pleasing to the eye, risk attracting insects and other vermin, which is not conducive to eating in a hygienic environment. Isn't it time that garden centres considered getting rid of all their plants and flowers and just concentrated on the cafe? Probably, yes, but I doubt it will happen in my lifetime. So... maybe you should just pack a picnic!

Let's make a 'pact' lunch!

Yes, I'm well aware that I misspelt 'packed', and when you hear the following heart-breaking story you'll understand why. One morning several years ago Ken Worthington and I were having a furious row over petrol-money payments for a civic walkabout in the Chesterfield area. I was dressed as Alderman Fitzwarren while distributing leaflets promoting a bouncy castle hire company, and Ken was maintaining that because the engagement involved me walking, I shouldn't have to be paid any petrol money. But I'd still had to get there, hadn't I? I couldn't have walked all the way to Chesterfield, done the walkabout and then walked back. Ken was behaving in a manner more crooked than that town's notorious spire!

"I tell you what, John," said Ken, letting out a sigh of resignation. "Let's make a packed..."

And then he hesitated. Was he going to finish the sentence or was he waiting for me to say the word 'lunch'? I would have loved to have made a packed lunch with Ken. It would have been a perfect way to heal the rift, and we were overdue a trip to Ladybower reservoir to check the level. As well as crab-paste sandwiches (and perhaps some peanut butter and jam ones?), we could have crammed my duffle bag with a six-pack of buffet pork pies that I knew we had in our pantry, a small Tupperware of salad, a couple of cans of Diet Sprite (it would have made my organ seat in the garage a bit lower, but no matter), two tangerines and two apples (obviously, I would have checked with Mary first even though it's my fruit bowl too so I wouldn't need to get permission really).

"Lunch? I'd love that, Ken," I said, trying to hold back a smile. What a lovely man Ken was. I felt bad for raising my voice to him.

But then Ken continued, saying, "Not yet, John. I've only just had my breakfast. So what do you think? Shall we make a packed...?"

He'd done it again! I was about to say "Make up your mind, Ken!" when he continued with: "...to stop arguing over silly matters like petrol money? I said I'd make you a star when you signed with Kenny Music, and we're still on course to achieve that, although you're no spring chicken and time's fast running out for you, as I'm sure you realise…"

I'd understood little of Ken's last few words, apart from 'chicken'. Was he proposing we pack some chicken drumsticks in the packed lunch? Nice idea, but HE'D have to provide them, especially if I was supplying the buffet pork pies. That was fair. And then suddenly, the awful truth dawned on me. Ken meant 'pact', not 'packed', and that's why he hadn't said 'packed lunch', because he didn't mean 'packed' – he meant 'pact'. Why would anyone say 'pact lunch', anyway? They wouldn't, because it doesn't make any sense at all!

That's the end of that story. Well, not quite. I left Ken's house at that point, went home and had four bowls of Sugar Puffs one after another as I was feeling a bit down, and not really thinking what I was doing. (I got through more than half a 2-litre bottle of semi-skimmed milk, so Mary wasn't happy.) Then I had a lie-down on my bed and faced the wall, and entered a fitful sleep. I felt such a fool, allowing myself to be duped by Ken, but I realise now it was because I'd not wanted to be arguing in the first place – I'd wanted to be in the Derbyshire countryside with my cagoule on, assisting Ken in the event that his Cuban heels became stuck in a muddy field.

There's been a lot of singing in this chapter, but what better way to pull yourself out of the doldrums, which I'm in now, I must confess, by singing a song which solves the dilemma of where to eat out good and proper: forget your house, forget the garden centre, and go and buy a portion of…

FISH AND CHIPS

How I love fish and chips
With mushy peas and those battery bits
That some call 'bits' and some call 'scraps'
We sat in the car and ate them on our laps

Mary had cod, Joan had plaice
And Ken's pickled onion had a very tart taste
It made him wince, and screw up his face
He loved it though – that onion was ace

We shared a giant bottle of pop
And we drank it down to the very last drop
The meal, we agreed, had been a delight
Then we wiped our greasy fingers on a handy wipe

And when we'd finished our fish and chips
Joan lit up one of her filter tips
Not in the car though – out on the cliffs
And I took the chance to grab forty winks

How we love fish and chips
With mushy peas and those battery bits
That some call 'bits' and some call 'scraps'
We sat in the car and we ate them on our laps

Oof, that's given me an idea: to go and eat my pudding – a Go
Ahead forest fruit bar and mini pot of (fibre-based) fromage frais –
while sitting in my Austin Ambassador, which is just parked in the
drive. I'll join you again shortly…

CHAPTER 14:

KIP, TIP OR PINGPONG?

Ooh, that's a funny title, in't it, but highly apt, as you'll see as the chapter unfolds. But before it starts unfolding I must tell you – there's been a development in the 'kidnapping of Mary and Ken'. As I suspected, they weren't kidnapped after all. The truth is far more upsetting! All the time I was sat on the bar stool eating my sandwich, Mary and Ken were living it up in Doreen Melody's camper van, along with Joan Chitty and Doreen herself. For some reason, Doreen has parked it right outside our house. When Mary bumped into Doreen at the local shops, an arrangement must have been made between the two ladies for Doreen to delay her return trip to her home in the Killamarsh area of the city, and come and visit our home instead.

I presume Doreen's van arrived while I was out in the garden spinning the lettuce, and – fed up of waiting for me to complete the task – Mary was enticed by Doreen to go and have her dinner in the camper van, and Ken followed suit. Who can blame them? I'd have liked to have had my dinner in Doreen's camper van too, while observing our house through the window and checking the gutters for weed growth, but I wasn't invited! I think we know why – because I was late spinning the lettuce, and because when I did, I splashed Ken with water droplets. Even now I'm clearly not welcome, as I'm sure they can see me sitting in my car in the drive, but no one is making any attempt to ask me to join the party. I do realise that I'm not very good company at the moment, but that's not my fault – it's because I'm writing a book, which makes you moody and distant and prone to erratic behaviour. Allowances ought to be made by the friends and family of sensitive authors, don't you think, readers?

What IS going on inside Doreen Melody's camper van? It looks like they're having a party. They're eating and drinking, there's raucous laughter being produced, and in Ken's case, occasional fisting of the air, but who can blame him? He's enjoying the life of

Me at the rear of Doreen's camper van – at a happier time when I was free to scale the sturdy chrome ladder, before climbing safely down again. (Note: three points of contact should always be maintained while ascending or descending a ladder.)

Riley – eating MY flan, in the company of a bevy of ladies. What a turnaround from an hour ago, when his strange salad fell onto our patio and his Afro was drenched with the spray from our lettuce. Well, I'll tell you what, two can play at that game – I'll have a party too. I'm going to pop in a Werther's Original and sing a song in praise of my very special car... it's a song I suspect many of you have been waiting for!

Y REG

I've got an Austin Ambassador Y reg, Y reg, Y reg
My Austin Ambassador Y reg
It's a car that I revere
My Austin Ambassador Y reg, Y reg, Y reg
Don't keep asking me why, Reg?
It just happens to be that year

Now, you may covet a Clio
Or a Montego
Marvel at the Mondeo
Fine, but not me, no

My Austin Ambassador Y reg, Y reg, Y reg
My Austin Ambassador Y reg
It's a car that I revere

Now you may be utterly sold on
Your Peugeot, your Proton
Your Mitsubishi Shogun
But I'll always dote on

My Austin Ambassador Y reg, Y reg, Y reg
Don't keep asking me why, Reg?
It just happens to be that year

I'd even say no ter
A Rolls with a chauffeur
A brand new Toyota
A Skoda? Give over!

(*Because I'm very happy with my current vehicle... more than happy.
And that's because it's – as I've already stated – erm...*)

An Austin Ambassador Y reg, Y reg, Y reg
My Austin Ambassador Y reg
It's a car that I revere
My Austin Ambassador Y reg, Y reg, Y reg
Don't keep asking me why, Reg?
It just happens to be that year!

It seems Mary isn't missing the lettuce I painstakingly spun – I can
see an open bag of washed salad leaves on the camper-van table,
and they're being enjoyed by Ken along with what looks like the
last piece of flan. No sign of Joan Chitty at this juncture, I note,
but... oof, tell a lie – Joan's just emerged from the toilet cubicle,
swaying slightly, glass of wine in hand. Ooh I say, that's not good
to observe mid-afternoon on a weekday. And now Joan's relieving
Ken of the last piece of flan, which he doesn't seem too happy
about, and not having had a single piece myself, I'm not happy
about it either! Oh well – leave 'em to it, I say. We need to crack
on with more domestic dilemmas...

Kip, Tip or Pingpong? (Please explain!)

Yes, I will, gladly. You see, wherever you decide to have your
lunch, upon its completion there's always a fresh dilemma to
face: do you settle on the sofa for a much-needed nap, but risk
incurring the wrath of your partner, or do you attach your trailer

to the back of your car and take a consignment of green waste to the recycling centre as you promised you would? Or do you ask your partner if they'd like a game of table tennis? There – I think you'll agree now that the unusual title for this chapter was bang-on. In fact, if you can think of a better one, I'd like to hear it!

John's Explanatory Note: Regarding the ability to nap away from your home: yes, I realise there's no sofa in a chip shop! However, if you've eaten your fish and chips in a car, simply adjust your car seat to a reclining position (having first deposited the wrappers in a nearby bin or you'll stink your car out) and then have a nap. I'm tempted to have forty winks now, readers, but I must keep writing!

John's Extra Explanatory Note: If lunch was at the local garden centre, why not take a siesta reclining in one of the garden swings? For a more private bedchamber, climb up to the mezzanine level of the Hansel and Gretel chalet and kip there, although don't be surprised if you're disturbed by children, who may clamber all over your body and incorporate you into their game, possibly casting you as a sleeping giant.

The negatives of napping

Being mistaken for a giant is one of them, but normally you would choose to take a nap at home, wouldn't you, and although it's lovely drifting off with the telly on low (and the occasional sigh of the dog wanting you to get up and take them for a walk –

169

which reminds me, I must take our Scottie dog Kirsty out shortly), there are serious negatives to napping in a domestic environment. Firstly, if you promised to go to the tip, or do some DIY for your partner, e.g. fixing the rotary washing line because it's spinning at a funny angle (that's what Mary has asked me to do today, you see), then they might rouse you roughly, with unkind words and maybe even a light prodding in the tummy, but hopefully instead it will be with a cup of tea and a Tunnocks!

Missing the salesman's call

Even if no one knows you're having a nap, what happens if you're asleep when the doorbell goes and you miss an unsolicited call from a conservatory salesman? How will you cope knowing you've missed out on a fascinating chat about dwarf walls and rear box guttering with someone in a smart suit? Luckily, I was awake when the salesman called last month and we had a long chat in our storm porch, although when I told him our maximum budget for a conservatory he said he'd have to go away and think about it. Don't leave it too long, Brian… sorry, I can't remember yer second name!

––––––––––––

John's Explanatory Note That Is Really A Warning!: If a salesman calling himself Peter Cornelius calls round, tell him to go away – you're having a nap. He's a slippery conman, and unfortunately a friend of Ken's, who will try and sell you a carriage clock that normally retails for £139 for £15, which sounds like a bargain but it'll probably conk out the next day. He also does a three-pack of small men's singlets which Ken says have proved durable and retained their shape well despite repeated washings, so hmm… maybe I'm being a bit harsh on Peter Cornelius? I don't know – the jury's still out on that man.

––––––––––––

What happens when you've elected not to have a snooze, but you still feel sleepy?

This is a very common dilemma and it can come on at any time of the day, but for me between 2 and 5 p.m. is when I'm most likely to suddenly drop off. Once the teatime quiz shows come on the telly, I'm more alert, but it's never easy before then. If it proves too difficult to resist the lure of the sofa, then so be it. Have a little nap, as long as you can get away with it. If Mary's popped out to empty the bin, or Karen or Joan Chitty calls her on her mobile for a chinwag, I know I'll have a few minutes at least. If they do catch you asleep, you could always say the dinner they've just cooked you has given you a poorly tummy and you're sleeping it off, or – even more deviously – say that the meal they cooked you was so delicious that you couldn't stop thinking about it, and so slipped into a reverie, which became a snooze!

The curious tale of the deaf artist dog thieves

Ken, as you know, is one of my next-door neighbours, but the lady who lives on the other side, Mrs Bond, is my other next-door neighbour, and she told me recently – while she was hanging out her washing, and I was checking that a fence-post cap I'd replaced was still preventing moisture ingress to the vulnerable fence-post end – that a couple of fraudsters are known to be operating in our area. Their scam is highly unusual: they knock on your door pretending to be a deaf couple with a painting for sale. Then, while you're looking at the painting, they run off with your pet dog! Oof, you wouldn't want to open your door to that situation, would you? You'd be better off sleeping right through their villainous call, or at least pretending to be asleep. But hang on – what if your pet is old and toothless with extremely bad breath, and it's costing you a lot in vet's bills (like a certain Scottie dog)?

And what if the painting they leave behind when they run off with your dog turns out to be worth millions? It's not a bad trade-off, is it? You'd be mad not to answer the door to that!

A trip to the tip

The other day Ken Worthington disturbed my nap by calling round, and thinking it was a salesman, I foolishly answered the door to him. He was offering me a small bookcase for nothing, as he was having a clear-out. A kind offer but one I declined as the bookcase looked simply too small to fit any DVDs into. I feel bad now because I could have taken it off Ken's hands and delivered it to the local tip, or recycling centre, as they're now called. I do enjoy hooking up my trailer and driving to the tip, where special skills are required:

> Special Skill 1: You need to be fleet of foot and able to change direction suddenly to prevent bumping into or being trampled on by someone carrying a sofa on their back whose peripheral vision may be impaired.

> Special Skill 2: You need to be mentally tough to handle the rough-and-tumble of tip activity. Sometimes those men in the hi-vis vests start shouting in a way that could intimidate the faint-hearted. But in fairness, they have to shout to be heard above the sound of all the video recorders being hurled into skip 4 (electrical), and often raucous pop music can be detected coming from somewhere, reminding me of that scene in *Apocalypse Now* when the soldiers have gone crazy and all sense of law and order is missing.

As a younger, fitter man than Alan the Opera Singer, who often asks me to deposit his green waste for him, I can cope with all the hurly-burly at the tip. After a while I forget I'm just a member of the public, imagining myself as a competitor in *It's a Knockout* (whatever happened to Arthur Ellis?). It's like you've been specially chosen to come and get rid of your household waste, and you feel a lovely kinship with the other tip users, especially if they've got a trailer too. However, if you hesitate in your mission, one of the men in hi-vis will approach you and say, "What've you got in there, buddy?" Then you may feel like you're in one of those police programmes on TV where they're arresting criminals, which brings me on to a very modern dilemma, though not a very domestic one, so it doesn't really belong in this book. But so what? Let's discuss it, anyway.

The terrible pressures on today's police

Doesn't it amaze you how policemen nowadays manage to combine their job of arresting criminals with their new role as TV personalities? I don't know how they do it, but somehow they do. They're super-cops, in every sense of the word. Think about it, readers: the policeman (or policewoman) has to describe what they're about to do to the suspect for the viewers at home, and then they have to carry it out on the suspect, e.g. tasering them or putting them in a headlock, while repeating to the suspect what they're doing to them AS they do it! Their coordination has to be spot on. THEN, they have to tell the viewer what's going to happen to the suspect next, having first explained it to the suspect, WHILE holding them down AT THE SAME TIME as presenting their best side to the camera, because – as they have to remember at all times – they're making a TV show as well as clearing up Britain's crime rate, and it has to look good, or ratings will slip, and that would be criminal, I'm sure you agree!

To be fair, there's a lot of pressure on the suspect too, because they'll know, either from past experience appearing on the show or from watching the programme themselves, that their face is going to be all blurry in the programme, so they need to keep their head fairly still, otherwise it's difficult for the TV editor to obscure their face in the editing process, I would imagine. So it puts massive pressure on both the suspect and the bobby in what is already a high-pressure situation. It can't be easy for any of them! Hats off to the suspects (can the quality of their TV performance be taken into consideration by the judge? I'm guessing not), and hats off to the boys in blue – not that they wear hats any more. And yet they need them more than ever, as none of them have much hair these days, it seems, and on a chilly night in Pontefract town centre they must be freezing!

Every man has his sport – and mine is table tennis! Note the grimace of concentration on the player's face as the ball hurtles towards his waiting bat!

Pingpong pangs

What I'd like more than anything else right now – even more than a snooze – is to indulge in one of my favourite pastimes with my wife, Mary, because to be honest, we don't do it half as much as when we were newlyweds or even courting. You've guessed it – I'd like to have a game of pingpong with Mary! I've got a feeling if I asked her right now she'd say no, because she's still cross with me for taking too long to spin the lettuce and drenching Ken with the spray. I might ask her later when things have calmed down a bit, and we can put the extra leaf in the dining-room table. Ooh, it'd be lovely. You see, we absolutely loved playing pingpong when we were younger. When we went on our honeymoon to Whitby we were at a complete loss because there was nothing to do really, apart from walk up and down along the cliff path. But we couldn't find a table-tennis table anywhere!

Before our children Darren and Karen came along, Mary and myself attended table-tennis training at the YMCA on a weekly basis. Mary had the sponge bat and she'd be attacking, and I had the hard bat and I'd be stood well back from the table, adopting a defensive style. Ray Pashley, the coach (he was an exceptional player and even played for South Yorkshire once when someone was ill) used to walk round the table giving advice and helping you improve your stroke, and sometimes he'd just watch us, and when the rally was finally over he'd wink at Mary and say, "Another long rally there, I see, Mary?" Oh, they were such happy days.

But Mary doesn't like playing pingpong with me any more, even when she's in a good mood. The reason? The rubber on her bat has become badly perished, and I think this has knocked her confidence. Ooh, it's a shame cos I'd love to stretch a net across the middle of our dining table and give Mary a good thrashing... oof, that came out a bit funny, but I hope you know what I meant there.

I'm going to go and knock on Doreen Melody's camper-van door shortly and discuss camper-van dilemmas with her. But let's end the chapter with a song all about the joys of playing table tennis. It employs the highly apt 'Japanese Enka' (rhythm 67 on my organ), and it's called...

PINGPONG PANGS

Just because there's a net dividing us
Doesn't mean we cannot play with kindliness
As long as there's a score to keep reminding us...

That I'm the best (Ooh, I missed!)
My game is steady (I wasn't ready!)
My topspin serve (It seemed to swerve)
My bottom spin (will do you in!)

Pingpong pangs, ying and yang
The perfect game for two
Playing pingpong you can't go wrong
It's a pleasurable thing to do
Tennis is for fools, there's too many rules
And you need bigger balls as well
But pingpong pangs, my pingpong pangs
Are the pangs I long to quell

What's the score? Eighteen–twelve! Overture!
(*Over to you... geddit?*)
Nineteen–fourteen? This surely means it's war!
Is it deuce? No thanks, I didn't request a drink (*deuce = juice –
    obvious, that one!*)
If you want to see this shot you'd blinking better not blink!

For I'm the best (Ooh, I missed!)
My game is steady (I wasn't ready!)
My topspin serve (It seemed to swerve)
My bottom spin (will do you in!)

KIP, TIP OR PINGPONG?

Pingpong pangs, ying and yang
The perfect game for two
Playing pingpong you can't go wrong
It's a pleasurable thing to do
Tennis is for fools, there's too many rules
And you need bigger balls as well
But pingpong pangs, my pingpong pangs
Are the pangs I long to quell

CHAPTER 15:

THE LAWN NEEDS MOWING, BUT I NEED A NAP (AND OTHER EXTERIOR DILEMMAS)

I'm not sure I've the energy to go and ask Doreen about camper-van dilemmas. The truth is, despite having to do the rotary washing line – and I've changed out of my slippers into a stout outdoor shoe in readiness – I'm tempted now to stay in my car, recline the seat and have a nap. I AM tired, having written more than half a book since I got up. That's pretty good going, isn't it, readers, but have you read it as quickly as I've written it, I wonder? I doubt it very much! But hey, let's put my achievement in perspective: that Barbara Cartland, she'd have written two or three whole novels by this time of the day, wouldn't she, if she was still around? I don't think she can be – it's a long time since she was on Russell Harty in her long pink frock.

But what do you do when there's a job that needs to be done but you can't be bothered to do it? It's a dilemma that all of us encounter on a daily basis. Whether it's mowing the lawn, walking the dog, washing up, even getting out of bed, sometimes we'd rather stay where we are, doing nothing (apart from sucking a sweetie and reading the *Exchange and Mart* – except you can't do that any more because they stopped printing it in 2009).

———————

John's Explanatory Note: But it doesn't stop you reading old copies of the legendary marketplace mag and imagining owning a faulty oil-filled radiator, a bag of rust-resistant grub screws, or even a scuba-diving gas cylinder – at 2009 prices!

———————

By this time tomorrow I'll have finished writing this book and be on to other exciting projects, such as trying to write a smash hit for Clannad, or little Leo Sayer. Ooh, I'd love to see the plucky songster make one more big dent in the top ten before he retires, and why shouldn't it be with one of MY songs he achieves this feat? But right now, I really must go and fix the rotary dryer. Or must I...

Should you do the nasty or the nice jobs first?

The way to approach this dilemma is: do you eat your cabbage first, knowing you've got a nice juicy sausage still on your plate to enjoy? Of course you do – unless you just eat the sausage and leave the cabbage? But you then risk getting into serious trouble, and it's the same with not doing the nasty job. You've got to do it at some point or your partner will turn against you, and ultimately you might not get sausages on your plate, just cabbage! So my advice is, do the nasty job first and leave the nice job till last.

You can't see from this shot but I suspect I'm still wearing my slippers. No problem as I'm enjoying a well-earned snooze, and am in no position yet to venture outside to test moisture levels on my lawn.

My favourite DIY job is power-washing the outside of our wheelie bins, but I've a terrible feeling I did it last week, so it doesn't qualify as a nice job I can look forward to. "Don't you mean the inside of the wheelie bins, John?" No, I don't, actually. Well, you should clean both – the inside, obviously, on a fortnightly or at least a tri-weekly basis, but the outside, that gets dirty too, you know, with grime from car exhaust fumes and other airborne debris which becomes affixed to the plastic, and it should be cleaned on a bi-monthly basis, so I've a good few weeks to wait before I can do it.

How dry must a lawn become before you can no longer use 'the grass is too wet to cut' as a valid excuse for not mowing it?

This is a huge dilemma that has affected husbands, particularly, up and down the land ever since lawnmowers were invented, and ruined many a Sunday for them (and their wives), but I'm afraid I can't really help you solve it. Only YOU can determine if the grass is still too wet for cutting, but I suspect in most cases it's perfectly dry, and you're just being lazy. I'm right, aren't I? Don't beat yourself up about it, but why not take preliminary steps to prepare for the task of mowing? Turn off the TV, get up off the sofa, pop outside and get the mower out onto the lawn at least, or even just open the shed door, as this will make removing the lawnmower later that little bit easier.

Peruse the sky for approaching rain clouds, and – if you still have sufficient mobility in your lower half – bob down on your haunches to examine the grass for evidence of moisture. I suggest you also use this opportunity to check that the grass is long enough to even warrant being cut. Perhaps you mowed it yesterday and have forgotten? In the event of this happy situation, return to the house and resume your position on the sofa. Give yourself an extra pat on the back if you forgot to change out of your slippers when you went into the garden — why, your feet are already suitably attired for placing back on the pouffe!

Halfway (house) to heaven

We don't have a lawn, as I've already stated, because a good few years ago we had the foresight to have it concreted over to create a glorious maintenance-free space. But back in the eighties I used to mow our little patch of grass, and I also used to cut a large lawn for the halfway house using our electric lawnmower, with the aid of my fifty metre extension cable. The halfway house has for many years now been run by Lesley, a lovely lady from Louth, Lincolnshire. Oof, that last bit had a lot of words beginning with 'L', didn't it, readers? And they were said in sudden succession in the same sentence. (Hang on, I think I've just done it again — sincere apologies, readers!)

In return for me mowing their lawn, I used to borrow their electric typewriter so I could type my letters to record companies, which I'd then post along with a cassette tape of my latest songs. Sadly, I don't mow the halfway house lawn any more (or borrow their typewriter... well, I've got Ken to contact record companies directly on my behalf, although I don't think he's done that for a long time — hmm, I shall have to have a word!).

Lesley uses a contractor now to mow the lawn: a couple of beefy lads come once a fortnight in a transit pickup van dressed in hi-vis clothing (and not just a skimpy yellow tabard like the one I have to trim our hedge). We're talking full-body orange suits and helmets with visors that give them an impressive military quality — you half-expect to see them with a semi-automatic weapon but, thankfully, they don't seem to possess one. But they do have a big powerful mower. Well, one operates the mower, and the other has a strimmer to do the lawn edges and they're, ooh, ever so quick. My goodness, twenty minutes and they're all done, equipment

Me standing fully erect inside my garden shed. If it was a Hansel and Gretel chalet I wouldn't be able to do this, although – being a shorter man – Ken Worthington would have no problem, I suspect.

back in the van and they're sat in the front on their mobiles having a vape. It's difficult to see them from the road but I notice every twenty seconds or so a thick coil of white smoke will fly out of the van window. It's not unlike a dragon breathing fire, I suppose, but it's not that similar either. And do dragons even exist? "Yes," claims my grandniece Michaela, but she has them all over her lunchbox, school bag and even pyjamas, so she's been brainwashed into believing they exist, hasn't she? She's going to be seriously disappointed in later years when she finds out the truth!

Roger from the halfway house

Roger – again, I don't know his second name, I'm terribly sorry – was a long-term resident at the halfway house who used to watch me cut the grass silently, his eyes boring into me as he sat at his window. Sometimes Roger turned the air blue because he was angry about having a collapsed spine, Lesley said. In the seventies he was a wealthy solicitor, you see, who had an E-type Jag and a succession of dolly birds, but then his back went, he turned to drink, his business failed and he was shunned by his family. That would make anyone want to turn the air blue, don't you think? And yet in moments of mental clarity, Roger would still dispense useful legal advice such as, "The wife has the right to do that, but the husband can still do this, etc." I can't remember exactly what the advice was, and although it was interesting, it was of no practical use to a happily married man like me.

Ooh, hang on, he's at the window. I don't believe it – Roger is there in his wheelchair and he's gesticulating wildly, while turning the air blue! "Roger, I thought you died in 2003. Keep your voice down and get yourself back to the halfway house! Your wheelchair is scuffing our carport posts, so back away! DO NOT RAISE

YOUR VOICE LIKE THIS IN A QUIET RESIDENTIAL STREET! DO YOU HEAR?"

"John? JOHN!" shouts a familiar voice, and I open my eyes to see the big round face of Joan Chitty at my car window.

"Goodness me, Joan!" I reply, smacking my lips, which I usually do when I've just woken up. "I think I nodded off there, Joan."

"I think you did, love," replies Joan, who has now walked round and opened the passenger car door and is attempting to climb into the seat beside me, but she's going to sit right on top of an empty fromage frais pot. Oof, she has!

"Ooh, that's better," says Joan, with a sigh. "I only disturbed you because you were twitching a lot, and shouting. I thought you might be having a nightmare."

"I was, Joan, so thank you for waking me up," I tell Joan, gratefully. "I was dreaming about Roger from the halfway house, and it was obviously a dream because he died in 2003, but in my dream he was alive and well and damaging my carport."

"Was he, indeed!" says Joan, chuckling, although – just as she found Mary going to buy sweeteners amusing – I wonder how she could find Roger damaging our carport a laughing matter?

"How are things in the camper van?" I venture, deciding not to accuse Joan of having a warped sense of humour.

"We've been having a smashing time," replies Joan, but then, shaking her head, adds, "but Mary and Ken have still not forgiven you for ruining their lunches. Because you did, didn't you, John? That was naughty of you."

Joan wags her finger at me and gets quite close to my face. Oof, I can detect drink upon her breath, and her breathing sounds a bit raspy. Clearly she would benefit from sucking a Locket, and Joan might be just in luck there, as I'm sure I have one loose in my trouser pocket.

(Sweet) Talking with Joan Chitty!

"Joan," I say, struggling to reach into my trouser pocket to retrieve the cough sweet, "I've got something for you in my pocket which I think you'll appreciate."

"Ooh, what makes you think I'm interested in what's in your trousers, Mr Shuttleworth?" replies Joan with a cackly laugh.

"You haven't seen what it is yet, Joan," I reply, struggling to locate the sweet.

"Oof, it's stuck," I eventually say, and instead open my glove compartment, revealing my bag of Werther's Originals.

Joan immediately grabs one and begins to unwrap it. It won't help her raspiness, but should sweeten her breath, which is, frankly, filling my car with alcoholic fumes!

"You don't mind, do you, John?" asks Joan, but she's already got the wrapper off the sweet and it's in her mouth before I can answer that. But I don't really mind because I'm about to ask her a big favour…

"Joan, I need your advice on domestic dilemmas."

"Ooh, do you?" replies Joan, sucking on her sweet, and pulling down the passenger visor to check her reflection in the mirror – yes, the Austin Ambassador does boast this feature.

"Mary's not being very cooperative," I continue. "Earlier, I asked her to help me out, and she gave me short shrift, Joan."

"Ooh, I see," replies Joan, gravely. "Well, you need to pick your moment carefully with a lady, John. Besides, you've been annoying her, so she'll be punishing you. You kept her waiting earlier so now she's keeping YOU waiting. Your dilly-dallying with the lettuce spinner made the flan go cold. Luckily, Doreen has a mini oven and so was able to heat it up in her van. Ooh, it was delicious!"

"I'm sure it was," I reply, slightly miffed, before unwrapping a Werther's myself and popping it in my mouth. "But I've been thinking, Joan, maybe I've been asking the wrong woman. Maybe it's YOU I should have been turning to in the first place."

Joan looks at me quizzically and says, "Go on, John, I'm listening…"

"After all, you've been a dinner lady almost as long as Mary, and your experience on the job has been more varied than Mary's — you've been on supervising duties AND custard…"

"Custard?" interrupts Joan, frowning.

"Yes, custard," I reply, "whereas Mary has only ever been on mixed veg. What I'm saying is you're more experienced in domestic affairs than Mary, so you're the right woman to offer me guidance."

"Do you really think so, John?" says Joan, sucking hard on her sweetie.

"I do, Joan. Can you help me out with my dilemmas?"

"Dilemmas in the bedroom, I take it you mean, John?" says Joan, coughing slightly.

"Well, yes, absolutely, Joan," I reply, excitedly. "We can start in the bedroom, and then we can move to other rooms in the house. I'd like to explore every area, if that's all right with you, Joan?"

Joan looks out of the car window in silence. She appears to be thinking hard about whether she's prepared to help me with my book. It IS asking a lot, I suppose, but then again Joan hasn't got much on at the moment — like Mary she's not at work because the schools are on holiday — and she lives alone with no dependants to rush home for. Ooh, I hope she does help me, because Mary's been pretty useless, it must be said, and despite having weak wrists, Joan may be able to suggest some ironing and possibly darning dilemmas. Or something like… "Should tracksuit bottoms be painstakingly folded and hung in the wardrobe, or hurriedly discarded in a heap after being worn?", that sort of thing.

Turning to me, Joan asks softly, "And where do you propose we do this, John? Right here in the car, or would you prefer to go somewhere more private?"

"Here in the car would be absolutely fine," I reply. "But, Joan…"

"Yes, John?"

"It might be best NOT to tell Mary what we've been doing, just in case she gets a bit funny about it. She might do, you never know."

"I think it would hurt her dreadfully, John. It's very important that she never does find out what we've been up to."

"Well, she'll find out when she reads the book, obviously."

"You're going to write a book about it?" asks Joan, her eyes widening. Then she chuckles again. "Ooh, John! I didn't know you were such a dirty devil!"

Although Joan's last comment has puzzled me, she seems fairly keen to help, and sensing she just needs a little cajoling, I add, "Look, I'm writing a song for Leo Sayer tomorrow, so, if it's all right with you, we should get down to business right away!"

"Ooh, John… you know I want to, but this is all so sudden. You've got to give me a minute to think about this," says Joan, breathlessly.

Joan seems conflicted. It's like she wants to help me, but something's stopping her. Why is she making such a big deal out of it? It's only advice on a couple of domestic dilemmas. Joan crunches hard into the Werther's, and finishes it far too quickly. Then she reaches into my glove compartment for another, which I personally think is a mistake – her taste buds will be saturated with the flavours of the sweet she's just had, and to have another now could prove an empty experience. I decide to tell her so…

"Joan, I think you should wait a while before you put it in your mouth and suck it."

"Now, stop it, John!" says Joan, appearing outraged now for some reason. "What ARE you like! Oh, I can't believe I'm doing this. I'm suddenly feeling like a vulnerable schoolgirl!"

"That's totally understandable, Joan," I reply, kindly. "You've probably not done anything like this before, have you?"

"Well..." Joan appears to be thinking, and then, smiling wryly, she says, "It's certainly been a while!"

"Now," I continue, sensing Joan's renewed enthusiasm for the project, "we can go as slow or as fast as you like. I'm recording everything on my dictaphone."

"Ooh, you ARE a kinky devil, John Shuttleworth!"

"Pardon? You've lost me there, Joan. Now, let me try and give you an example of a bedroom dilemma, just to get your juices flowing. Let's see, erm..."

I notice Joan has reclined her car seat, leaned back and closed her eyes, and she seems to be puckering her lips. Perhaps she's doing that to help her concentrate on thinking of dilemmas. I'd better come up with an example to get her started...

"Erm... sock sorting, Joan. Should it be done the moment you spot a sock on its own, or should you let them build up and earmark a weekend a month hence to pair up stray socks in your sock drawer?"

"I'm sorry...?"

Joan has opened her eyes and is looking at me blankly, and has even momentarily stopped sucking the second sweetie, which is a good thing. If she still has the wrapper it wouldn't be too late for her to remove it and save it for later. Doh, she's sucking it again. Never mind. But she seems confused by that bedroom dilemma. I'd better give her another example...

"Or... what do you do when you want a sip of water in the middle of the night? Do you switch the light on and risk waking your partner, or do you reach out in the dark for your glass or tumbler and risk knocking it over onto the floor, the almighty clatter of which would surely rouse and anger them?"

"Hm, I see," answers Joan, sighing and suddenly sounding a bit sad and sleepy. "I don't know the answer to that one. I can't say I ever thought about it very much, John."

"Well, you should have done, Joan," I reply, "It's important. Or it could be a kitchen dilemma, I suppose, such as… what do you do when your partner wants to store the Swarfega under the sink or even in the garage, but you'd like to keep it on top of the sink next to the washing-up liquid for immediate access?"

"Oh, Joan, what an old fool you are!" sighs Joan, before clasping her forehead, and banging it hard repeatedly with her fists.

"You're being too hard on yourself, Joan," I reply, kindly. "I'm sure you'll think of something shortly. Here's another… what's the protocol when a dishcloth reaches the end of its natural life? Do you throw it away or do you put it under the sink and let it become a floorcloth? I know what I'd say – it should become a floorcloth every time! It's a natural progression. But many is the occasion I've had to fish an old dishcloth that Mary has discarded out of the bin and place it under the sink so it can begin a new life as a floorcloth. And the dilemma doesn't stop there, Joan. I then have to check on a daily basis that the new floorcloth is still there under the sink and hasn't been thrown away again by Mary. If it has, I have to fish it once more from the bin, and if it's become soiled in the bin by coming into contact with some food waste, it has to cleaned thoroughly before resuming its role as a floorcloth. It's exhausting work, Joan, as is hunting for the Swarfega – if Mary's removed it from the draining board and hidden it on a high shelf in the garage. So, have you any thoughts of your own yet, Joan? Er, Joan…?"

But Joan, it seems, has nodded off. I can't believe it. She's fast asleep, and is even starting to snore slightly. Oof, what's she done that for? She's more useless than Mary!

Oh well, maybe now is an opportune time to sing a ballad all about Joan and her rather sad single life (although she does have some family living in the Gleadless area, I believe). It's written from Joan's perspective and contains rather personal information about a former partner, but if she's asleep hopefully she won't hear. I'd better sing it softly. Here goes:

MY EX RAY

My name is Joan
And I'm all alone
This Christmas time
But I've got my phone
I'll be at home
I'm sure I will be fine
But I wish I could see my ex, Ray
Not cos I've broken a bone
But cos he was the only man I loved
And he left me on my own

I used to have a budgie called Les
He sang the sweetest song
And when he died, the tears I cried
But to get another budgie seemed wrong
And I wish I could see my ex, Ray
Not cos I've broken a bone
But cos he was the only man I loved
And he left me on my own

Yes I wish I could see my ex, Ray
Not cos I've broken a bone
But cos he was the only man I loved
And he left me on my own

Ah, that's rather sweet, in't it? And Joan slept right through it. Having said that, Joan is now making a strange gurgling sound. I hope she's all right... Hang on, I've just remembered, she went to sleep with a boiled sweet in her mouth. That's not wise, in fact, it's very dangerous – she could choke on it.

"Joan?" I say, in a worried tone, and then I shake her by the shoulders and shout loudly. "Are you okay?"

John's Explanatory Note: This is one of the key early stages of ascertaining if someone is choking and requires artificial respiration, as recommended by the International Association of Drilling Contractors. I discovered their marvellous website accidentally one day while searching online for a new chuck for my Makita cordless drill.

But there is no response apart from a sleepy smile from Joan, which might actually not be a smile but a grimace of pain as the sweetie chokes her and she slowly slips into unconsciousness. Oh blimey, I need to try something else...

John's Explanatory Note: Abdominal thrusts (the Heimlich Manoeuvre) mentioned earlier in reference to Julie Satan and Ken will be difficult to achieve given our current seated position, as will 'five slaps on the back', also recommended by the NHS, and the American Red Cross.

With Joan still lifeless, I decide to move on to the next stage of resuscitation techniques – to open the victim's airway by tilting the head back with one hand while lifting up the chin with my other hand. Then I will need to position my cheek close to the victim's nose and mouth and look down towards the victim's chest for signs of breathing.

I'm doing that and, erm… I've noticed that my wife, Mary, is standing outside the car looking in, and behind her is Ken Worthington. That's good news, obviously, as they can open the front passenger door and help me in the resuscitation of Joan. But why aren't they doing that? Neither Mary nor Ken seems to be wanting to help. In fact, Ken's covering his hand with his mouth and guffawing, which is an appalling reaction to someone's misfortune. Mary's reaction is equally baffling – she's just standing there with her arms folded, looking daggers at me.

John's Explanatory Note: I've seen this expression before. Mary used to look this way at our grandniece, Michaela, whenever she helped herself to fruit from our fruit bowl without asking first, which you should only do at Christmas time. (And even then, I think you'll agree, readers, there is only a small window of three or four days when it is deemed acceptable.)

"I can't believe it! Well done, John!" shrieks Ken Worthington, opening my car door, and patting me vigorously on the back.

"Wrong back, Ken!" I say, encouraged that Ken at least is trying to help, but baffled that the idiot is slapping MY back and not Joan's, SHE'S the one with the sweetie potentially lodged in her windpipe!

"I really didn't think you had it in you!" continues Ken, in a jubilant state. "Now this has happened I feel totally confident in approaching a publisher with your book."

"Well," I reply cautiously, "if you're considering sending it to a company that specialises in medical publications, I must stress that I didn't get to follow through on any of the advised techniques. For instance, I was in totally the wrong position for abdominal thrusts."

Ken doesn't reply, but looks skyward with an exultant leer on his face while punching the air repeatedly, and oof... Mary has just stomped off back to the house! I'm not sure what's going on here, readers. Joan, meanwhile, has just opened her eyes, coughed slightly, and carried on sucking her sweetie. I'm glad she's fine but I have a nasty suspicion that the biggest domestic dilemma in this book might be my own. And this one might be trickier to solve than any I've tackled so far!

CHAPTER 16:

SMELLS LIKE WHITE SPIRIT

I'm stood outside on our patio and I've just completed an appraisal of the faulty rotary washing line. What was Mary on about? It's fine… but she's not currently available to be consulted on the matter. Mary's in the bedroom, I presume having a clothes sort-out. I can certainly hear the banging of wardrobe doors and dressing-table drawers being opened and shut. Oof, I can hear her struggling to close a drawer now. It seems to be stuck. That's a dilemma that pops up occasionally, isn't it, readers? Let's tackle it immediately.

Jammed jrawers, jimjams and jumpers!

Oof, taking a bit of licence with the subtitle there, but it gives a fun quality to what is otherwise a rather depressing issue. Usually the result of someone rushing to open or shut a drawer, as is Mary at the moment – what DO you do when a drawer becomes jammed and no amount of pushing or pulling will free it? Sometimes, there is still sufficient space to squeeze a hand in and extract (or indeed deposit) items of clothing, and the temptation is to leave the drawer in its miserable state and carry on with your life, never ever fixing it. But to do so is extremely naughty and you must resist the urge. You see, undue stresses are being put on the chest carcass by the trapped drawer, twisting it out of shape, so you must untrap the drawer immediately. But why, oh why, did you let the drawer get stuck in the first place? If only you'd stood square on to the drawer, legs well apart for maximum stability, and bent your knees and back so your arm trajectory was low enough to be at the correct level to undertake a successful drawer-opening or closing movement. If only you'd done that, all of this would have been avoided. Ah well, you'll know for next time!

But back to the rotary dryer... there is no dilemma here because the angle of rotation seems to be fine. Perhaps Mary overloaded one side with several of Darren's wet shirts, and balanced it only with a pillowslip, so it spun at a funny angle. I'll keep monitoring the situation over the next couple of days before I rush out with any tools. I'd like to tell Mary the good news but I sense she doesn't want to be disturbed right now.

Instead, why don't I sing a song all about the virtues of DIY, which will inspire everyone to get cracking and solve all those awkward DIY dilemmas!

ODD JOB

Face the facts – your fascia has cracks
And your gutters and downpipes are leaking
Look at your roof – to tell the truth
It's a wonder the neighbours are still speaking
Your fence needs creosoting
It'll probably require a second coating
Your house is offending
The rest of the neighbourhood, you should

Stop clashing, and start blending
Improve your home and then you can invite your friends in
For a chinwag
But first I suggest those curtains would look best in a bin bag
You will hobnob
Proud in your palace, which now only requires the odd job

How I wish you had a satellite dish
Without one you stick out like a sore thumb
I'm amazed you're not double glazed
It's pricey, but so nice when it's all done
Please don't be insulted
And while you're at it get your lawn ashfelted
Your house is offending
The rest of the neighbourhood, you should

Stop clashing, and start blending
Improve your home and then you can invite your friends in
For a chinwag
But first I suggest those curtains would look best in a bin bag
You will hobnob
Proud in your palace, which now only requires the odd job!

Ooh, I'm in the mood for an odd job now. I could power-wash the wheelie bins, but as we've already established, they don't really need it until the scheduled date of Thursday week. We've no lawn to cut, as you know. The rubber seal on the door frame of our storm porch has been checked for signs of perishing, plus any grit deposits that could prevent a perfect seal with the door, and – not found to be wanting in any way – has been realigned. I even squirted some WD40 on the hinges of our Karen's rabbit-hutch door, just in case the hutch is ever used again.

Plonker's reconditioned engine

Earlier I told you that after Karen's rabbit died the hutch was used to house a reconditioned engine belonging to Plonker for his Datsun Cherry. He's taken it away now and anyway Plonker drives a scooter, so I'm not sure what happened to the reconditioned engine. I miss it terribly. No, not that much, but I did used to like studying it through the chicken wire, especially when it was raining, to see if the engine casing got wet – it rarely did. I suppose looking at a rabbit would have been more fun, but at least the engine required no feeding or cleaning out!

Guinea pigs (don't they know it's rude to stare?)

A guinea pig would have been even more fun than a rabbit because, well, guinea pigs are not frightened to establish eye contact with humans and, once established, maintain it, indefinitely. Put it this way, if you or I had a staring competition with a guinea pig, the guinea pig would surely win. This I have not found to be true with any other mammal. For instance, if I stare at our Scottie dog, Kirsty, for ages, eventually she looks away and licks her fur or pretends to be catching a fly, but a guinea pig wouldn't do that. How do I know? Because I had one as a schoolboy growing up in the Derbyshire village of Bamford and it would watch me continually as I cleaned out its cage.

John's Explanatory Note: Bamford is near Ladybower reservoir, where I go regularly to check the level. I'd like to have popped there today but there aren't many domestic dilemmas to be found on the banks of a reservoir. The other interesting fact about Bamford is that TV presenter Peter Purves once lived there when his parents ran the local public house, but I don't remember seeing him. (Before my time, I reckon...)

I'd be interested to hear David Attenborough's opinion on the guinea pig's staring abilities. Mind you, he's too busy saving the planet to consider such a trivial matter. How about Tony Soper – remember him? He's gone a bit quiet, so perhaps he might be able to spare the time to comment. Having said that, Peter Purves has gone a bit quiet too, and he used to sit and stroke a dog a lot on *Blue Peter* so he might have a view! What do you think, readers?

It's gone a bit quiet upstairs too, although, oof... I've just heard Joan Chitty raising her voice to Mary. Perhaps Joan's gone up there to help Mary decide and is currently trying to persuade Mary NOT to get rid of a particular blouse or skirt, and I'd wholeheartedly agree with Joan. ALL of Mary's wardrobe is extremely tasteful and worth hanging on to. Either that or Mary is trying to steal Joan's new tights, and Joan's having none of it. But Mary wouldn't do that, even if Joan's tights were small enough to fit her...

Oh well, it seems I'm not required to do any DIY this afternoon, which is a rarity. It's still a bit early to be thinking about preparing our tea, or is it? I should check with Mary, as occasionally she likes an early tea. I wouldn't mind one, as I'm starving, having missed out on the flan. Speaking of an early tea – I've got a song all about that which I'd like to sing now, and as you'll hear it's chock-full of domestic dilemmas!

EARLY TEA

We had our breakfast at the usual time
We were washing the dishes by a quarter past nine
Coffee break was neither early nor late
We sat down for our dinner at 12.58
That's when she dropped the bombshell on me
A late arrangement for an early tea

A late arrangement for an early tea
She had to be somewhere by six, you see
I began preparations immediately
I was peeling potatoes by a quarter to three
My afternoon plans consigned to history
By a late arrangement for an early tea

The hurly-burly of an early tea
Purely surly I should surely be
But when you're faced with the urgency
Of an early tea – it's an emergency!

I was laying the table at a quarter to four
Spinning the lettuce outside the back door
Spinning it more – until my arm was sore
But all for a purpose so the pain I ignore
It was almost exciting, I was happy to be
In a late arrangement for an early tea

A late arrangement for an early tea
She had to be somewhere by six, you see
Then the telephone rang, and she talked for a while
When she came off the phone, she announced with a smile
"There's been a slight change of plan. Happily
I'm not going out now, let's have a late tea!"

I should really check with Mary to see what time she's going out to Bums, Tums and Thighs with Joan Chitty, but she's still up in the bedroom and the way those two are arguing they won't be going out anywhere together tonight!

The 'early tea' phenomenon

Normally we have our tea around 5.15 to 5.18 p.m. I realise that's unfashionably early for a lot of younger people, but there'll be some older readers now gulping in disbelief at how late we're dining, as they'll be sitting down for their tea at 4.30 or around that time. It's a fact that as you get older you DO have your tea earlier and earlier. Several years ago I remember we used to have our tea at 5.30 p.m. on the dot, the whole family sitting down together (ah, happy days…), and yet I'd be a liar if I said I'm not looking forward to a few years hence when I just know Mary and I will smash the five o'clock barrier! Oh yes – the older you get, the earlier you do everything – get up in the morning, have your breakfast, your dinner and your tea, and of course, go to bed. "Bring it on", is what I say!

A late tea

There's some arty student types who live in the big house across the road from us. That's the house whose bins I thought the fox was going through, until I realised the sound was coming from Mary's nose. In the past I'd have been taking Kirsty for a walk around 8 p.m., 8.05 – it's earlier now I'm getting older (7.35ish) and it suits Kirsty too as she prefers an earlier routine now she's getting on a bit – and I'd see these young people just sitting down to have their tea. At that time, I ask you! We'd have had our tea and washed up many hours before and they'd be just sitting down to a big spread. You know, with candles and everything – it was like Santa's grotto in there! Then upon my return from the walk (around 8.40, 8.44, occasionally as late as 8.50!), they'd still be at the table. Oh, they'd have finished their tea but they'd still be sat there, you know, they wouldn't have got down. They'd just be chatting and playing with bits of paper. Funny old world, isn't it!

Ken's mildewy chairs

It certainly IS a funny old world. I'm back in the garden and I've just spotted Ken Worthington on his patio, bent over his two old wicker chairs, and it looks like he's FINALLY cleaned off the mildew!

"Ken!" I shout excitedly. "Can I just say it's lovely to see you've finally cleaned the mildew off those chairs, and done it so quickly!"

"There's a simple reason for that, young man," replies Ken, with a sly grin. "It's because it WASN'T mildew – it was green crayon, and it came off extremely easily. NOW do you believe me?"

"I suppose I have to, Ken," I reply, somewhat suspiciously.

"Yes, and I trust the matter's now closed and we can move on with our lives," says Ken, before leaning forward, and asking lasciviously "How's the bonkbuster coming along? Any more steamy episodes I can tantalise the publisher with?"

"Don't be so silly, Ken," I reply, tutting. "But you've reminded me – I've a steam cleaner in the garage that you could borrow to finish those chairs off, should it be required. But I'm not sure it is. They're looking lovely, Ken. Well done, sirrah!"

"Thanks, John," replies Ken, bashfully, before giving one of the chairs a slight flick with his duster.

"Ken?" I enquire, casually. "What product did you use, by the way, to clean your chairs?"

"Nothing at all," replies Ken. "I just let the rain wash the mildew away."

Did you hear what Ken just said? I did, and can't let his answer go without comment!

"Aha!" I cry, shaking a finger at Ken. "You just said 'mildew'! So you're admitting after all these years that it WAS mildew on the chairs and NOT green crayon!"

Ken stands stock still, silently turning bright red, his mouth slowly opening and shutting, as his head moves from side to side – only very slightly, but very rapidly, if you can imagine that? I've got him, and he knows it!

But suddenly I feel a bit mean for taunting Ken year after year about the mildew on his chairs. Why did I keep on doing that? Surely it was enough for me to know privately it was mildew. Why do I need to hear my next-door neighbour and sole agent admit it was mildew and not green crayon as he's always insisted? Maybe the green crayon story was a way for Ken to keep a precious memory alive – that of his nephew's visit. I don't think Nathan has visited since, and can you blame him? Ken has no toy box, or even a sweetie tin to amuse a child. Just a packet of crayons, of which one was presumably the colour green?

John's Explanatory Note: Although it was definitely mildew, couldn't Ken be speaking the truth? Isn't it possible that there WAS green crayon on the chairs, which in time got covered up by mildew? No – wax crayon is waterproof, and mildew would not affix itself to a waterproof non-absorbent surface, so Ken's a big fibber, and he knows it!

Look, the thing is, we all know now that it was mildew, because Ken's admitted it publicly. It's on record. It WILL be in the book, unless, oof... Ken edits it out, of course! That's what he'll do when he proofreads my manuscript. Ah, so what, let him.

"Just to say, Ken, that although you've admitted publicly the crayon was really mildew, please feel free to erase that fact when you proofread the manuscript."

"Thanks John. Yes, I might do, actually, because it was a slightly embarrassing admission," replies Ken, breezily.

"Ooh, Ken," I say suddenly. "I've just realised something."

"What's that, John?" replies Ken, as he sits down on one of his super-clean wicker chairs and takes a sip of Malibu.

"It's a shame those wicker chairs are now clean, because the dilemma of whether to clean off the mildew or not could have fitted very nicely into this chapter. The angle would have been: 'Should you leave mildew on your garden chairs, or should you go to the trouble of cleaning them but thereby missing out on valuable "sitting drinking Malibu" time?'"

"Ooh, I see," exclaims Ken, cocking an eyebrow. "Yes, I can see that's a dilemma that might be of interest to, erm... one or two people."

"It would, Ken, I'm convinced of it," I say, as I notice that Ken's face is returning to its normal colour, and thank goodness, because it was totally scarlet before. "Why don't I pop over the low boundary wall and rub some mildew or garden soil, perhaps, into the chairs – temporarily, of course? Just for long enough for us to discuss and hopefully solve the dilemma."

But then as I start to climb over the wall that separates our two properties, Ken holds up his hand and says, "That's quite far enough, thank you! Stay where you are!"

What's going on? And what's Ken going to do next? He seems to be about to say something. Yep, here it comes...

"John Shuttleworth... You must never touch my chairs or even come near them ever again, is that understood?" says Ken with a strange calmness. "They're all I have left from my marriage to Rhiannon."

"Rhiannon, who was…" I start to explain, but Ken cuts me off.

"…who was the harpist who accompanied me on *New Faces* in 1973, when I came LAST!" Ken spits out the final word so violently that a little bit of spittle is visible on his chin, just as there was a hint of saliva at the side of Tony Hatch's mouth when he crucified Ken all those years ago on that legendary TV talent show.

"But," Ken continues as his face softens into a beaming smile, "if you're needing a domestic dilemma for your book, John, I'll gladly give you one. I've just been painting my pantry shelf. I spilt curry powder on it some time ago, and it stained the shelf yellow. It wouldn't wash off so I decided to paint over it with white gloss paint. I've just been doing it, in fact, but I didn't get round to cleaning the brush, so I've left it in a jam jar of soapy water by the kitchen sink. My dilemma is: how do I finish cleaning the brush when really I want to be sitting in my garden enjoying a Malibu?"

"Ken!" I whisper, aghast. "I don't believe it! Have you really gone and put a brush covered in gloss paint in a jar of soapy water? The dilemma is actually whether we can save the brush in time, but I believe we can. Lead me to the brush, Ken, this instant!"

"Hang on, what do you mean – save the brush? What have I done wrong?"

"Oh Ken, surely you know that you should have cleaned your brush in turps substitute or white spirit, if you were using an oil-based paint, which being gloss I assume it is?"

Ken looks at me blankly, blinks and then takes another sip of Malibu. He's reminded me of another occasion years ago when I asked him a simple question, and his response was… well, I can only describe it as…

Ken's 'soapy rag' blunder

I was getting a muffled sound in playback mode on my cassette recorder (even when the Dolby button was disengaged), and I wanted to play the greatest hits of the Nolan Sisters that I'd just bought from Sue Ryder for 20p. Ken had popped round and I asked him how you should clean your cassette-tape heads, just to check that he knew really, but his ridiculous answer made me realise he didn't. Ken said, "You take a rag or dishcloth and douse it in soapy water, and then you rub it on the tape heads." I was utterly flabbergasted. You and I know, readers, that what you actually use is isopropyl alcohol, which you dap carefully onto the tape heads with a cotton bud. When I told Ken that he turned pale, shook his head and blurted, "Well, nobody told me that, John. Nobody told me…" Pathetic!

And Ken's doing it again now. He clearly doesn't know how to clean a paintbrush, and needs to be educated. Luckily, I've written a song which dispenses practical instructions for paintbrush cleaning. It was initially written to instruct my daughter Karen after she fell into the same trap Ken has foolishly entered. She'd been painting her bedroom skirting board purple with an oil-based gloss paint and afterwards placed the uncleaned brush on the sink where, left unattended, the bristles would have gone hard in a very short space of time, ruining the brush for ever. The song is called 'Smells Like White Spirit', and when I told Karen the title she said, "Someone's done that one already, Dad!" She told me the name of the group – Neonarnia, or something? They've gone a bit quiet, apparently, and they made a grave error because they called their song, 'Smells Like TEEN Spirit'. Obviously, they didn't look at the label on the bottle properly when they called it that. "It's white spirit, lad!"

Curiously, their song is quite similar to mine musically, although mine is a lot better, obviously, and their advice for brush-cleaning is, well… not very helpful. I'm going to end the chapter by singing my version. It's got a bit of a 'heavy metal' feel – I hope you're all right with that, readers? If you like, during the song, you can put your hands on your hips and rotate them as you pitch your head forwards and backwards violently, but I don't recommend that, because every time your head stops suddenly and then flies back the other way, your brain will follow just a little bit later. Did you know that? I first heard that on *Tomorrow's World*. As I recall, presenter Michael Rodd was crouching on his haunches when he told us. It's a bit worrying, knowing that, isn't it? It makes you not want to move your head at all! Not that Ken's worrying about that – he's already playing air guitar as he walks up and down the low boundary wall, thrusting his neck in and out like a strutting cockerel. Oof, Ken, no! Calm down and watch those Cubans on the wall. Ooh no, it's all right, he's wearing his Moroccan slippers!

SMELLS LIKE WHITE SPIRIT

Nobody rushes
To clean out their brushes
When they've been using an oil-based paint
But it's essential
Don't be mental
Clean out your brushes without complaint

First wipe off excess paint on newspaper
Then soak in white spirit – don't leave it till later
Immerse to the root of the bristles you've gotta
Then finally rinse through in soapy hot water

You can relax now
You have done it
Though your whole house smells of white spirit
Smells like white spirit
Smells like white spirit
Mm, that's lovely
Smells like white spirit

Nobody rushes
To clean out their brushes
When they've been using an oil-based paint
But it's essential
Don't be mental
Clean out your brushes without complaint

Smells like white spirit
Smells like white spirit
Now your whole house smells of white spirit
Smells like white spirit
Smells like white spirit
Oo, that's lovely
Smells like white spirit!

"Right Ken, I'll go and save your paintbrush now," I tell Ken, hopping over the low boundary wall before marching towards his back door.

"Thanks, John," replies Ken, a little out of breath, as he flops back into one of his wicker chairs and picks up his glass of Malibu. "And in return I'll try and forget that you drenched me earlier, and ruined my edamame bean salad!"

"It's a deal, Ken!" I reply, pleased that I'm starting to make friends again with those nearest and dearest to me. It's just Mary I need to worry about now...

CHAPTER 17:

TWO MARGARINES
(THE ULTIMATE DILEMMA?)

I'm well aware that many of you will have bought this book purely to find out what to do if you find two tubs of margarine – open and in use – in your fridge. I'm sorry to have kept you waiting for this advice, but I hope the wait hasn't been too distressing, and that you have appreciated the solutions to all the other domestic dilemmas I have pointed out up to now. And there are a good few more to come before the book ends, I do assure you!

The funny thing is, I've just opened our fridge door to get the milk out for a cup of tea for Mary (yes, my wife is talking to me again, which is marvellous news, and I've just completed a DIY task which should sweeten marital relations still further – I'll tell you about that shortly), and as I opened the fridge door I thought for one horrible second that we – the Shuttleworth family – had more than one tub of margarine in the fridge. But then I realised that what I'd thought was the second tub of margarine was actually a carton of reduced-fat cream cheese, and so – phew! – we currently only have one tub of margarine on the go.

But several years ago, the nightmare happened and we really did have two tubs of margarine in use. To backtrack just slightly, we'd done a big shop at Netto the previous week and had purchased two tubs of Utterly Butterly as it was a 2 for 1 deal, you see.

John's Explanatory Note: This wasn't the same trip to Netto when upon our arrival we saw a lady in a Vauxhall Corsa 'nutting' (to coin a phrase) the steering wheel. We initially thought she must be cross with herself because she'd forgotten a major item off her list. But then we looked again and saw that in fact she was just trying to pull her car seat forward!

Why do the blinking supermarkets still persist with 2 for 1 deals when they know it can lead to such domestic misery? (Or 3 for 2 deals – that's potentially even more of a nightmare scenario.) Anyhow, we arrived home and I helped Mary unpack the shopping as I often do, because I'm a modern man, as you know! There was at that stage a tub of margarine still in use, but there was only enough in it to spread on a few slices of bread. Still, it remained in the fridge as the 'tub in service' for a further three days, as I recall. The two recently purchased and unopened tubs went into the salad box at the bottom of the fridge, beneath a 400 gram pack of honey roast ham, but readily available to be brought into service when required, i.e. when the tub with only a bit in was exhausted, or 'used up' I could have said, but I chose not to.

Five days later that tub had been removed from the fridge (and washed out and placed in the recycling bin? I don't think people did that sort of thing back then – I'm sorry to say, I think we just chucked it), and the first of the two recently purchased tubs of Utterly Butterly was enjoying its new life as the ONLY margarine in service in the Shuttleworth household. Well, that's what I thought...

I don't want to get into the blame game but, well… it's totally Mary's fault. For reasons best known to herself, she decided not to hunt thoroughly for the 'tub in service' before going to the bottom of the fridge and taking out the second tub, opening it and spreading some marge on a Ryvita. In her defence, Mary has always maintained that she looked for but couldn't find a 'tub in service', so opened up the second Utterly Butterly. Indeed, a thorough examination of the fridge's contents just after the terrible discovery of 'two margarines on the go' revealed that the first tub was well hidden by a corn-fed chicken and a large jar of low-fat mayo. Some call it mayonnaise, don't they, which used to really annoy me because it sounds too wordy. Put it this way: 'tuna mayo' has a fantastic ring to it, but 'tuna mayonnaise' sounds silly to me.

John's Explanatory Note: I believe there's a county in Ireland called County Mayo. Now, I don't want to offend the residents of that fair county, but to me that sounds silly. Surely it would be better if they renamed it 'County Mayonnaise'. They'd get loads more visitors, I bet you, so I do hope the Lord Mayor (or Lady Mayoress) of Mayo is reading this and taking note!

As I was saying, it is just possible that Mary didn't see the open tub. But maybe she could have looked a bit harder? Anyway, it happened and we got over it and life goes on – but that's not how it felt at the time…

The nightmare scenario (as the key events unfolded)

A few minutes after I'd first made the grim discovery I went in search of Mary and found her in the hall wiping out the little dish that we use to put chocolate Brazil nuts in on special occasions. There were no nuts in it at the time even though it was in a way a special occasion, but special for ALL the wrong reasons!

"Mary?" I said in a hushed voice – I didn't want to alarm her. "Something's happened that we need to sort out."

I took her to one side, guiding her by the arm as I explained the situation fully, and she put down her micro-cloth and the surface spray on the telephone table so I knew she was taking the matter seriously.

"But don't worry, love," I continued, "we can sort this out. We'll get over it. It seems a big problem, but it doesn't have to be."

I could hear my heart pumping fast and I was getting quite breathless as I carried on: "I've had a good think, and what we'll do is this: we'll scoop a little bit of margarine from the tub that's well established and put it into the tub that was opened in error. We'll smooth it over and then when it looks full, reseal it and place it at the bottom of the fridge underneath the lettuce." (The packet of ham had been eaten up by then – by Darren mainly, as I recall – and a triple pack of midget gem lettuces was now in its place, although I think at the time I may have described it to Mary as a single Webb lettuce, but when you're in a state of shock it's hard to remember things precisely – that's my excuse, anyway.) "All right, Mary?" I asked, squeezing my wife's hand in solidarity. "And then we'll just forget about it and get on with our lives."

John's Explanatory Note: A triple pack of midget gems = three lettuces on the go! Isn't that even more of a nightmare scenario than two margarines? Well, technically yes, but those lettuces were unopened – they were still bound together in their cellophane wrapper and shouldn't be regarded as three separate lettuces, and anyone who does so is being pedantic and petty!

I naturally assumed Mary would be pleased with my plan, but do you know what? She just looked at me and said this: "Don't be so stupid, John. That's far too complicated. It doesn't matter. We'll just have two tubs on the go. It's fine. Matter closed!"

And then she picked up her cloth and her spray and went upstairs, I think to shake out the duvet, leaving me reeling at the foot of the stairs. I couldn't believe what she'd just said. For a while I didn't move from the spot, I was utterly floored by her reaction. And then I found myself walking up and down the lounge carpet. I think I was in that thingy state – is it fight or flight? I suspect a psychiatrist would've had a field day if they'd been there, and I wish they had been – to examine Mary and find out what the heck she was playing at, because I was very upset with her reaction. Very upset. You know, I just couldn't accept her decision, but deep down I knew I had to. And I'll tell you something: I slept very badly that night. Because there should only be ONE tub of margarine on the go at any one time, shouldn't there? You know I'm right, readers. And if you don't know that then I'm sorry but YOU need your head examining by a psychiatrist! (But I realise it's quite pricey for just a single session so you probably won't bother, will you?)

———————

John's Explanatory Note: Why are they so pricey – psychiatrists? Is it because they always have a box of expensive tissues? I know they get through a lot because they pass you one as soon as they think you're going to cry, don't they? I remember seeing that on an episode of *Ally McBeal*, but it can't be just that. They have expensive leather sofas too, so maybe it's that.

———————

I remember once we had two Daddies sauces in the fridge, and there can only be one Daddy, can't there! But joking aside, two of any open food or drink product in a fridge is asking for trouble, and, thankfully, Mary responded positively on that occasion to my concerns by chucking one of them away (there was hardly any left in it so that's probably why she did). But years after the 'two margarines' incident, I still think Mary should have taken my advice more seriously, and it's upsetting to note that she's never fully apologised for the emotional upset that her dreadful decision caused me.

That's why – even though Mary is only upstairs and so probably within earshot – I have no hesitation in singing this song loud and clear, and I hope you'll do the same!

TWO MARGARINES

Two margarines on the go
It's a nightmare scenario
Two margarines in my life
Two margarines to spread on my knife
Two margarines, but which one
Should I use to butter my scone?
It's a dilemma second to none

Two margarines on the go
It's a nightmare scenario
Two margarines in my life
Doesn't seem to bother my wife
She's the one who ignored the first
And opened the second, which began the curse
Of the two margarines
Is there anything worse?

(*Well, as I write, it's possibly the protracted negotiations of the B word – you know, to do with leaving the EU, and as you read it might still be ongoing, oof, I hope not! But apart from that, there's nothing worse, is there?*)

TWO MARGARINES (THE ULTIMATE DILEMMA?)

Two margarines on the go
It's a nightmare scenario
Two margarines in my fridge
It's enough to end a happy marriage
Two margarines, how I long
For the day when there's just one
My wife says, "You're a lunatic, John!"
But two margarines?
It's like a bad dream...

Yes, there should only ever be one. Having said that, you CAN have two tubs on the go – as long as one is clearly marked 'For Baking Only'. So now you know!

"You ARE a lunatic, John," comes a familiar voice from the landing.

"Hello Mary," I say to my wife as she comes down the stairs. "Here's your cup of tea – I'll just put it in the alcove next to the little bowl of Miniature Heroes."

––––––

John's Explanatory Note: We're currently trying out a different treat to chocolate Brazil nuts. It's not a permanent switch, just a trial, and we'll see how we get on with them, but so far they're proving very popular – especially with Darren, who helps himself to two or three at a time, and this ultimately may prove to be the undoing of the Miniature Heroes, and force us to return to chocolate Brazil nuts, which Darren doesn't like that much, but I do!

––––––

"Your sweetener is already in, by the way, Mary."

"Thank you, John," says Mary wearily as she picks up the tea, and she stands on the stairs with her mug staring at me for a long time, which is nice, as she doesn't seem to do that very often these days.

"You've been a long time in the bedroom, Mary," I say. "Is everything all right? Did a drawer get stuck? I take it Joan has gone home now?"

"She has," says Mary, and then there's another long silence. "When are you going to finish this book you're writing, John? Because I've found today quite difficult. In fact, to be honest, you've given me a big dilemma."

"Ooh, Mary," I reply excitedly. "Will you please share it with the readers, because it would be marvellous to have your input even at this late stage in the book?"

But Mary doesn't answer. Instead, she carries her mug down the stairs, goes into the kitchen and closes the door behind her.

I sense she doesn't want me to join her, so I get the dog lead off the hook in the storm porch and prepare to take Kirsty out for a walk. She's getting on a bit now, our Scottie dog, so she doesn't need to go far. And she doesn't seem that bothered to be going. Did you hear me? I just described our dog YET AGAIN as a Scottie dog. I'm making a grave error calling her that, because Kirsty's NOT a Scottie dog. She's not black – she's white. Not that colour matters, of course, but she's a West Highland terrier and should be described as such. It's something I've got wrong for years now, and I humbly apologise to Kirsty and any other West Highland terriers who have ever been wrongly described as Scottie dogs. Or, for that matter, any Scottish terriers who have ever been called West Highland terriers! And what better way to show I'm truly sorry than by singing a brand new composition to Kirsty as I walk her round the block.

"I'm just taking Kirsty out for a walk, Mary," I tell Mary, poking my head round the kitchen door.

"About blinking time!" says Mary, fluffing up some mashed potatoes.

"Did you notice I've repaired the mug tree?" I say, gesturing to the worktop where a perfectly balanced, stable and vertical mug tree is sitting. Mary looks at it and seems mildly pleased!

"Oh, how did you fix that then?"

"The same way that you make shepherd's pie, Mary... I just did it!" I say, and I think about giving her a wink, but I don't think we're friends enough yet for that. "I'll see you shortly, love."

"Don't be too long, Kirsty'll get tired."

Ooh, Mary seems a bit more like her old self. That's good, and I'm delighted to note she's making her signature dish for tea. I'll tell you all about that in the next chapter, and before we end this one with that musical apology to Kirsty, I should explain about the mug tree, because of course, I didn't 'just do it', and it certainly wasn't done in the same way Mary makes a shepherd's pie – I don't know why I said that, as the techniques used were wildly different. It was the result of much experimentation, and I'd like to tell you what I did so that you know what to do yourself next time your mug tree goes wonky.

How to repair a wonky mug tree

Well, you could just place mugs on different branches of the tree to redistribute the weight until the mug tree sits perfectly vertical, but that will only be a temporary fix, readers. As soon as a mug is taken off the tree it will lean horribly again, as ours had been doing for the last few days, and getting steadily worse. And remember – the sight of the mug tree leaning might dissuade a prospective mug user from using that mug, and make them hastily replace it and choose another mug. But still the mug tree will be leaning, and so the dilemma of which mug to choose will go on and on – and you'll never get your cup of tea made!

The way I fixed it was to empty the tree of mugs entirely, so that it stood mug-free – naked, you might say, but, oof, that's a bit of a strong word to use – and then sort out the problem, which I did. "What WAS the problem then, John?" Well, the joints were loose, weren't they! That was the problem, so I simply got my mallet from the garage and lightly tapped in all the branches until there was no movement. I then sanded the mug tree base, having first chiselled off a lump of heavily congealed fat in one small area of the base (the result of a cooking accident by Darren, late at night, I'll warrant!), and this clearly was affecting the base's levelness, and so compromising the mug tree's ability to stand vertical, proud and tall (well, it's quite diddy really, but you know what I mean). But hey, I fixed it, and Mary's pleased I did. And that's enough for me. Right, I'm off for a walk with Kirsty, who has been waiting extremely patiently. Good girl! Here's the song I promised you, Kirsty, and I trust you'll listen too, readers, as you accompany us on the walk:

KIRSTY IS A WESTIE, NOT A SCOTTIE

(Ideally to be sung in a silly Scottish accent, like Stanley Baxter used to do on the telly, especially when he was dressed as an old lady. Do you remember? I don't really, it seems so long ago now.)

Kirsty is a Westie, not a Scottie
I knew that when we bought her as a puppy
But at some point I forgot
Started calling her a Scot
But she is not and must think I am potty

TWO MARGARINES (THE ULTIMATE DILEMMA?)

Kirsty's not a Scottie, she's a Westie
Mary knew but never tried to correct me
For years this joke has run
People must have thought me dumb
And Kirsty's come to shun and even detest me

Kirsty is a Westie, not a Scottie
Everyone knew but no one tried to stop me
It's an error I regret
Repeating it to my pet
And everyone I met
While on a walkie
And to get it wrong for so long is very naughty
For Kirsty is a Westie – not a Scottie!

Oof, I think Kirsty enjoyed that. So much so that's she given me a little present on the pavement! Luckily, I remembered to bring a poop bag...

John's Explanatory Note: Dog owners: please always carry a few little bags when you walk your pet. If you forget and your dog answers the call of nature on the road, you must go back home and get a bag. There is no dilemma here – even if no one is around to see. Thank you for your cooperation!

CHAPTER 18:

YOU CAN'T GO BACK TO SAVOURY NOW (OR CAN YOU?)

I was well into my thirties before I tried Stilton cheese, and I only tried it the once, so it's a memory that's stayed with me. I was a guest at a wedding, and I'd filled up on so many different cakes and puddings at the buffet table that I'd had to loosen the waistcoat of my three-piece suit before I could sit down again. Meanwhile, my young attractive wife Mary was dancing to 'Dancing Queen' by Abba – hey, that proves it was a wedding, doesn't it? She was dancing in a group of several ladies, plus a little lad in a kilt whose dance steps were highly erratic and his presence dangerous to the safety of the group, in my view – although nobody seemed to mind, I couldn't believe it! Oh, plus the bride who was called Veronica, I think, or it might have been Vanessa? Some name beginning with a 'V', anyway. Oof, it's a poor do that I can't remember the name of the bride, isn't it? Vicky, was it? Hang on, we'll be here all night if we have to go through all the girls' names that begin with a 'V'. Mind you, I can't think of any more, can

220

you? Erm... Violet! No, it wasn't Violet. That's an old lady's name, isn't it? Well, back then it was. Plonker's sister Jade has just had a little girl called Violet, so names do come round again, eventually.

John's Explanatory Note: I heard Joan Chitty tell Mary the other day that the school caretaker's niece has just had a baby boy and they've christened him 'Derek', which is a name you wouldn't have expected to come round again so soon, is it? A baby called Derek, well I never!

Anyway, Veronica... I'm pretty sure it was Veronica. I'll have to ask Mary to verify but in order to do that... erm... Verity? The word 'verify' made me think of Verity, but you know, I really don't think it was that. That's a posh lass's name, and there was nothing posh about Veronica. Yes, Veronica... I think. Mary'll know, but we'll have to wait until she returns from Bums, Tums and Thighs to find out for sure. Yes, good news, folks – Mary and Joan have gone to their exercise class as normal. I thought they might be giving it a miss because of the raised voices I heard earlier, but clearly they've come to a cordial agreement. My hunch is this: Mary was going to give Joan a suitcase full of her clothes (I saw it on the bed when I came up), but then she changed her mind and Joan was understandably a bit miffed about her change of heart and words were exchanged. (Mary's unpacked the clothes again, I'm gratified to note, and I've put the suitcase back in the loft for her.)

Joan is due to drop Mary back home after the class in her Citroen Berlingo, in around half an hour, which gives me time to do the pre-bedtime checks around the house: putting the dog out, checking all windows are closed (on the ground floor this must include all window locks being fully engaged), closing curtains throughout the property and ensuring they're tucked in behind the radiators to minimise any potential heat loss. I've just done the lounge and obviously took extra care with the curtain behind Mary's pot shepherdess.

Anyway, if I MAY finish my story: after she'd had her dance with Veronica... or Vanessa, I'm now favouring Vanessa as the name, actually... erm, Mary went to the buffet herself and got a plate loaded with a selection of different cheeses and brought them back to the table. And she wanted me to share them with her, which I was initially resistant to because I really was stuffed, but I managed to nibble on a little wedge of Edam, because it's quite easy to digest, isn't it, that one? However, one of the cheeses on the plate was Stilton – the one with funny blue veins running through it. You know the one, I'm sure. It's mould, basically, so how on earth it falls within the guidelines of the Food Safety Act, 1990, beats me! But when I told Mary I'd never tried it before, she made me. And ooh, no, it was not pleasant. My taste buds were shocked by the rich flavour – and so was I!

Why did I tell you that story? It was to illustrate a very important point: that once you've had your main course of meat or fish, or Hello Umi – is it called that? Our Karen raves about it, it's a Greek cheese, apparently, best grilled or fried. But anyway, after you've moved off your savoury course onto your sweet (and it's called that because it IS sweet, generally), well, you can't go back to savoury again, can you, and any attempt to do so is foolhardy in the extreme. I know some people – usually posh, well-educated folk – like to try and convince the rest of the population that we're wrong and they put themselves through what must be absolute torture by eating, straight after they've had their sweet, strange bitter fruits, cheeses and pickles, and goodness knows what else and I feel very sorry for them. Why are they doing it? It can't make them happy.

John's Explanatory Note: It can be no accident that people who undergo this strange ritual do so usually after they've consumed a large quantity of pain-numbing wines and spirits. Yes, this will soften the blow, I'm sure, and make the crazy transition from sweet back to savoury more bearable, but it's still baffling that they feel compelled to do it in the first place!

You can't go back to savoury – but I did!

The only time I EVER went back to savoury, apart from the sliver of Stilton Mary made me eat at that wedding, was at a school friend's party in Great Hucklow, Derbyshire. Not a million miles away from Hathersage? No, you're right there, but even closer to the village of Bradwell with its big cement works. Because it was a fine day we had a picnic in a nearby field close to my friend's house.

Great Hucklow is only a mile or two away from the Derbyshire and Lancashire Gliding Club, so on occasions during the picnic the sun would disappear briefly as a glider flew over the sun. It was a bit like a giant switching off his torch for a second and then switching it back on again, and I found it a little disquieting, but it didn't stop me tucking into the potted-meat sandwiches. Ooh, they were lovely, and I praised them to the mother of the lad whose party it was. But rather than be delighted about my compliment she just pursed her lips and said, "Well, don't eat too many, John, or you'll be sick."

John's Explanatory Note: Although I did have quite a few – possibly fifteen – remember that each sandwich was only a quarter of a slice of thin white sliced bread (although doubled up, i.e. two slices plus filling), so fifteen sandwiches equates to only seven and a half slices of bread – but ooh, that's quite a lot, I suppose!

Eventually, I'd had my fill of potted-meat sandwiches, and decided it was time for a fairy cake. (Mary will be pleased that I'm mentioning fairy cakes again – that's six mentions now, and there'll be more by the time this story is over, I'll warrant!) Anyway, all the other children had finished eating, and gone off to play 'dare' by leaping over the cowpats. But I just sat and watched them while eating a mini chocolate roll and hoping for another glider to fly over and briefly blot out the sun. (But it didn't, sadly.) Now then: do you remember those cakes that used to have a wrapper made out of rice paper? Well, I do and I assumed that the wrapper of the fairy cake was made of that, so once I'd finished eating the fairy cake, I started to eat the wrapper. But I soon realised it WASN'T made of rice paper – it was a wax-based greaseproof paper, and proved very chewy and not at all suitable for consumption.

I started spitting out the bits onto the grass, and the mother of the party host, who was clearing up around me, saw me do that and told me off and gave me a little smack on the wrist, which made me cry, but only a little bit. Did I feel betrayed by the lady whose sandwiches I had praised to the hilt only minutes earlier? I did slightly, but I wasn't traumatised or anything. At the time – once my mouth was clear of nasty waxy paper bits – I just carried on eating more cakes: a mint Viscount (you know, the green one), another mini chocolate roll, and finally a jam tart.

Wasn't I tempted to have another fairy cake? No, I wasn't. I WAS going to try a lemon curd tart – not because I wanted one, because by then I was absolutely stuffed – but to see how it compared with the jam tart, when the lady held up the plate of potted-meat sandwiches and said, "Do you want any more of these before I give them to the dog?"

You may find this difficult to believe, readers, but I reached out and took three more sandwiches (one and a half slices of bread), and as I got off the picnic blanket and went to look for the rest of the children, who by this time had disappeared, I ate all three of them, but without really thinking what I was doing. Still, I definitely ate them, crusts an' all, and as I moved slowly through the field, I started to feel sick. And then next to the stile, I WAS sick. Now you could argue that was because I'd eaten too much, but I reckon it's really because I went back to savoury, which you should NEVER EVER do, as I've already stated.

What to do when dinner guests are so fond of savoury that they can't go back to it… because they're still stuck on it. (i.e. They won't go onto their pudding!)

Before she went out to her exercise class this evening, Mary and I had tea together. It was shepherd's pie, which readers may or may not know is Mary's signature dish, and my favourite meal of all time. As a goodwill gesture to Ken Worthington to show I was sorry for drenching him with the lettuce spinner earlier, I had invited him to join us, and he had readily agreed. For a small man, Ken has an extremely hearty appetite, and as I observed him polish off his first serving of shepherd's pie, I was concerned that he'd be wanting more. But I didn't want him to have any because I knew it would have spoiled his appetite for his sweet – a lovely apple crumble from Herons (I defrosted it myself) with custard, plus evaporated milk (to be offered as an optional extra).

Shortly, I will explain a technique you can employ to dissuade greedy dinner guests from asking for second helpings. But first, let's remind ourselves of how greedy Ken Worthington can be, by singing a song I wrote after visiting a carvery with him and Mary in the plague village of Eyam, Derbyshire.

Before we do that though, I must just tell you something rather fascinating. We got a taxi there and back to the carvery. Ken paid for that which was very generous of him, but he was rolling in it at the time because another of his clients, Janet Le Roe, had just played Simple Simon in *Robin Hood* in Keighley. It wasn't Stan's taxi – I don't think we had the minicab card on the notice board back then – but anyway. When we arrived in the plague village of Eyam, I couldn't help but notice something: the meter had reached £16.70. Can YOU spot anything significant there, readers? No? Well, that's because there isn't anything significant. But if the meter had stopped just 5p earlier it would have registered £16.65. "So what?" I hear you cry. Well, what was the year the tailor brought the bundle of offending cloth from London to Eyam that caused the plague to decimate the population of that charming Peak District village? Think... think! That's right: – 1665. Eerie, isn't it! But before you marvel at this amazing coincidence, I have to point out that you're forgetting something: the taxi meter only advances in increments of 10p, so sadly it could NEVER have registered £16.65.

John's Explanatory Note: There's nothing to stop you, however, from purchasing £16.65 worth of petrol whenever you fill up at the Calver Service Station, just a few miles outside Eyam. I regularly do that, except it's quite tricky to stop filling up at exactly that amount, and more often than not I end up on £16.66 – the year of the Great Fire Of London!

Let us now bang our tankards in time as we sing 'Mary Had A Little Lamb'. Some of you may be thinking, "Ooh no, I'm not singing a nursery rhyme – that's childish!" While I understand where you're coming from, may I suggest you let the lyric establish itself and then you'll see that you were very wide of the mark in assuming it was a nursery rhyme!

MARY HAD A LITTLE LAMB

Mary had a little lamb
Green beans and new potatoes
I had tuna and sweetcorn flan
We served ourselves – no waiters

(*Because it was a carvery, you see...*)

Ken plumped for the shepherd's pie
I said "Ken, you're outrageous!"
For he had piled his plate sky-high
To eat it took him ages

We had a carafe of sweet white wine
And Ken had a gin and tonic
There was a giraffe for children to climb
Though no children were on it

(*Because it was a bit drizzly outside...*)

Mary had a little lamb
And that was her big folly
For she was famished when it came
To viewing the sweet trolley
A substantial main course would have made
A sweet unnecessary
As it was, she suffered 'Rigor Mortis by Raspberry'!

So — do you offer seconds, or don't you?

Well, of course you do. Not to offer seconds to a dinner guest would be rude. It's HOW you offer the seconds that's important, and determines how successful you will be in dissuading the guest from accepting them. Whatever you do, don't fall into the trap of saying "Would you like some more?" because that will put ideas into their head that it's an acceptable thing, and they'll almost certainly say (especially if they're a greedy-guts like Ken), "Ooh, yes, please!"

The crucial thing is to word the invitation in such a way that your guest is put off from having seconds from the start. You need to plant the idea that they don't really want any seconds, by saying something like, "So you're positive you don't want any more, Ken?" Normally this should be enough to dissuade them, but if you see them looking a bit disappointed or hesitating with their answer you need to jump in quickly, saying, "Pass me your plate, then!" Say it in quite a jaunty way to reduce any potential grumpiness or resentment from the guest, and once you have their plate put it straight in the sink or the dishwasher. Then you are free to say, "Well, I'M going to have a little more", but say it in a weary tone, suggesting you're making a sacrifice by having more, as you take your own plate to the stove and reload it liberally with as much as you want! Keep your back to the guest as you do so, and whatever you do don't establish eye contact with them at any point, or the pleading look in their eyes might soften you up enough to blurt out, "Oh, go on then, have some of my seconds!", or something equally foolish.

So, back to the meal earlier this evening… We had all finished our main course but only Mary had put her knife and fork together. Both Ken and myself had left ours in the time-honoured 'inverted V' position, indicating that we'd both like a little more. I had noticed — during a mid-meal visit to the sink to get the dishcloth to wipe off some gravy I'd spilt on my trousers — that while there was plenty of cabbage, supplies of shepherd's pie were alarmingly low, so realising that there would only be sufficient to provide seconds for one diner, at the end of the meal I said to Ken:

"So you're positive you don't want any more, Ken?"

I could see him looking crestfallen as clearly he DID want seconds, so I needed to follow it up with the next bit. But before I could say, "Pass me your plate, then," he said suddenly, "Well, I could manage a little more, if that's possible?"

Oof, I was so shocked that he'd broken protocol in this way by answering swiftly that I couldn't think what to say, so without thinking I said exactly what I was going to say if he hadn't said anything. I said, "Pass me your plate, then", and of course Ken did just that!

It was an awkward moment – Ken was holding his plate out to me and looking all eager, and there was me, not wanting to take it. I needed to think of something fast – a way to distract Ken and make him forget about having seconds. Remembering that Mary hadn't pointed out any food that might have landed on my face during the meal, but realising that there may be a deposit of some kind, I said to Ken: "Ken, have I got any food deposits on my face? Mashed potato on my eyelid? A gravy splash on my chin perhaps?"

Ken looked puzzled and said, without looking very hard, "No, you're fine. Please take my plate, John – it's getting heavy!"

My ruse hadn't worked. I needed to do better than that, so I suddenly went "Oooofff!" as if I had a terrible itch on my head, and began scratching it furiously with both hands.

It was quite pleasurable, actually, and so I closed my eyes for a few seconds, fully expecting to hear Ken say "Are you all right, John? Have you been bitten by an insect, perhaps?" But instead, I heard Ken say this: "Ooooo, THANK YOU, Mary!"

Can you guess what happened, readers? That's right – while I had my eyes shut, Mary had got up, brought the shepherd's pie dish over to the table and replenished Ken's plate. I couldn't believe it – it was piled high, just like at the carvery in Eyam! Mary was clearly trying to empty the dish as her spoon was scraping the edges and piling every last bit onto greedy Ken's plate.

"Hang on, Mary, aren't you going to save some shepherd's pie for ME?" I remonstrated, but Mary wasn't having any of it.

"There's plenty of cabbage if you want it. And there's apple crumble to follow. Besides, I think you should go to the bathroom and rub some of that insect-bite soothing gel on your head. Go on – it's in the cabinet."

"I'm fine now, Mary," I assured her, as I mournfully watched Ken tuck into MY seconds.

For a moment I felt sorry for myself, but after watching Ken struggle with his mammoth (ill-gotten) second helping, noticing his reddening face and the perspiration forming on his forehead and the mince dribbling out of his mouth (which he'd suck back in noisily before shovelling yet another forkful of MY shepherd's pie into his fat little mouth), I started to feel sorry for KEN! But this pity soon turned to disdain and then resentment as I realised he's a bit of a user, is Ken Worthington – always coming round to heat up his curry in our microwave, or asking me to come and unblock his kitchen sink.

John's Explanatory Note: A task I enjoy, to be fair – disconnecting the pipework and removing the trap before cleaning out all the grease, matted hair and other demetrius that's caused the blockage, before washing thoroughly the separate components – taking care to reseat the thin rubber washers during the reassembly.

Ken even gets Mary to iron his shirt if he has a celebrity charity dinner that evening. On one occasion a good few years back, it was a celebrity do in Youlgreave, Derbyshire where (Ken claims) Jimmy Tarbuck was the star guest, although to me that seems too incredible to be true – for a star of Tarby's standing to venture to Youlgreave! Apparently, the event was to raise money to buy boxing gloves for underprivileged youngsters, and at one point (Ken alleges), Tarby took Ken to one side and – after blowing his cigar smoke right into Ken's face and making an extravagant gesture in the air – said the following words: "If it happens for you, Ken, it's a great life. But if it doesn't happen for you – it's still a great life!"

Ken didn't really know what Tarby meant, and I don't either. (Do you, readers?) All I know is that if Jimmy Tarbuck had been at our tea table tonight and watched Ken steal all my shepherd's pie, he would have had to concede that it HADN'T happened for me that mealtime, and that for me – it WASN'T a great life!

Ken went back home to his bungalow a while ago and is sat in his lounge now in his big leather armchair watching telly. How do I know that? Looking through our lounge window I can see the back of his Afro, moving slightly as he tilts his head forwards or backwards, depending on whether he's having a sip of Malibu or putting his glass down, and then there's the occasional violent movement as he seems to jerk his whole head around in some kind of spasm. He could be laughing at the hilarious antics of Mrs Brown and her boys, but more likely – it'll be indigestion, and it blinking well serves Ken right!

I'm feeling calmer and more philosophical than I was earlier, readers. I've written nearly a whole book today, and I know I've upset a few people along the way. But I've made up with them again, and as I look around the lounge and take one last look at the back of Ken's Afro before closing the curtains on the darkening sky

I'm not sure what I was looking at here, readers. It may have been a group of disaffected youths on the street, or Ken eating a bowl of cereal while walking along the low boundary wall. Or I may have simply been admiring our car port!

– taking care not to get too close to Mary's shepherdess – I realise something very important...

No, it hasn't happened for me – I've not become very successful in the sphere of popular music (which remains my dream, incidentally). But on the whole, it's still been a great life. Tarby's right. I've got a loving wife and two lovely children, and we're a close-knit family unit, and tomorrow I shall get up early and go in the garage and start trying to write a hit for Leo Sayer. Or Vince Hill – mind you, Vince is getting on a bit and might not be that bothered any more about being chart-bound, but I am. It'd be lovely, having a hit, and then me and Ken might get invited to a celebrity charity dinner together, and I'd have to go up on stage and collect an award (maybe from Tarby himself!), and then say a few words. And I'd thank Ken for all his help, and he'd go bright red.

Perhaps the song should be for Lulu? She's not graced the charts for a while... or an exciting punk outfit like The Alarm? Michael Ball! Michael Crawford? Erm... what about Michael Bublé? Whoever it is, they should have a twinkle in their eye, and a zest for life like I have. Oh, I dunno... I'm getting a bit sleepy now. Time for bed soon, I think. I'll end this chapter (not the book, of course – there's a whole chapter on tooth-brushing dilemmas to follow!) by singing a song that some readers may consider my finest.

———

John's Explanatory Note: Apart from 'Pigeons In Flight', of course – the song that could have prevented Norway from scoring 'nul points' in the Eurovision Song Contest some years ago, if only they'd chosen it as the Norwegian entry. Perhaps I should send a cassette copy to Graham Norton (with Dolby on, obviously), and try and sneak it in there as next year's UK entry!

———

This song references all the dilemmas we've discussed in this chapter, and I shall sing it to you as I make myself a hot chocolate and take it upstairs, and await Mary's return...

I CAN'T GO BACK TO SAVOURY NOW

My wife Mary made a lovely shepherd's pie and peas
With carrots and gravy. Oh, and cabbage, as an additional green
I said, "That looks fantastic, love" and I tucked in hungrily
My daughter Karen did not – something I wish I had seen

For soon my plate was empty, I said, "Mary, is there any more?"
She said, "No, love, but it's treacle sponge for afters", and I said,
    "Phwoar!"
I'd had a couple of mouthfuls when I heard Karen declare
"I can't eat any more of this shepherd's pie, Mum."
Well, it filled me with despair

(*Cos if I'd known that, I wouldn't have started on my sweet!*)

But I can't go back to savoury now
That shepherd's pie was stunning
But I'm halfway through me pudding,
I can't go back to savoury now
My taste buds would go crazy
I can't go back to savoury now.

My tummy was in turmoil, I was panicked and confused
And as Karen's dinner grew colder, so did my sweet
For my pleasure in that treacle sponge was now massively
    reduced
By the sight of fluffy potato and glistening meat

YOU CAN'T GO BACK TO SAVOURY NOW (OR CAN YOU?)

Take this plate from me, Oh Lord, before I go insane
Should I press on with me afters
Or go back to me main?

No, I can't go back to savoury now
That shepherd's pie was stunning
But I'm halfway through me pudding
I can't go back to savoury now, oh no
My taste buds would go crazy
I can't go back to savoury now.

I can't go back, I won't go back
I'd love to go back, but I mustn't do that
I can't go back, I won't go back
Obviously I'd love to go back, but I mustn't do that!

At that moment I heard a sound – the scrape of knife on plate
As I watched Karen's dinner go in the dog's dish
My appetite now gone, my pudding suffered the same fate
I can only assume that this appalling outcome was God's wish!

I can't go back to savoury now
That shepherd's pie was stunning
But I'm halfway through me pudding
I can't go back to savoury now, oh no
My taste buds would go crazy
And I can't go back to savoury now
No, I can't go back to savoury… now!

CHAPTER 19:

TOOTHBRUSH TROUBLES

Well, Mary's back, and her and Joan are still the best of friends which is good to hear, although Mary gave me no exciting details about what it's like to travel in a Citroen Berlingo. I shall have to engineer a ride with Joan at some point, as the Berlingo is the only vehicle I'd be mildly tempted to trade in my Austin Ambassador for (or the Renault Kagagoogoo, which I've heard is very similar). I suspect some readers may be shocked to hear me say that, but you know, all good things must come to an end (like this book, which has only a couple more chapters to go, I'm afraid). Don't worry, I'm sure the Y reg has a few years left in her, although I was perturbed to discover water ingress to the glove compartment after the recent heavy rain. It was so bad that it managed to penetrate a poorly wrapped Werther's, mildly discolouring it (it still tasted delicious though!), and I guess that event has knocked my confidence in the vehicle slightly.

Things are back to normal with Mary too, I'm relieved to report. From the upstairs landing I can hear her in the kitchen doing the final night-time checks – switching off unwanted power points, calling Kirsty back in from the garden and bolting the door against potential intruders. I've not yet heard her empty the toaster crumb tray, though perhaps she did it very quietly? Right now, all is silent down there, apart from the comforting rhythmic whirring of the dishwasher which she must have just put on, and I suspect Mary's final task will be to run the micro-cloth one more time over the kitchen surfaces. I don't think we're going to hear her do that though above the noise of the dishwasher, unless the surface spray is employed, in which case we'll hear a succession of short hissing sounds.

Incidentally, my son Darren is back from his night shift at the off licence and my understanding is he's currently powering up his Xbox while he waits for his Super Noodles to soften. We've not heard too much from Darren (or Karen, for that matter) in this book, I do realise that, but, fret ye not – they're absolutely fine. Like all young people they like to lead their own lives and aren't too bothered about hanging out with their mum and dad. It wasn't always like that, of course, and I want to remind you of what a close-knit family the Shuttleworths really are by singing a song all about us. I'm going to perform it in the bathroom, where I am shortly to brush my teeth, so my performance will benefit (as it did earlier) from the slight echo provided by the shower tiles.

THE ISLE OF ARRAN

I've got a son called Darren
And a daughter whose name is Karen
Without them my life would be barren
Like living on the Isle of Arran

Now, Darren used to be a nuisance
But since he started work at the off licence
He's out until twelve, his hair is nicely gelled

And we get on really well
Yes, he's a true prince

Now, Karen plays the recorder
And composes pretty tunes to order
And when she was small, she threw some gravel at a wall
Though she thought she was alone, in fact I saw her

(*But I took no action, because that's what toddlers do, in't it…*)

Mary is my charming wife
We lead a very full life
As does my Scottie called Kirsty – she's dotty
When she scampers with her paws it drives me potty

(*Oops, I've just called her a Scottie again, sorry Kirsty! But yes, she likes to scamper on the cover of the* TV Quick, *and once she damaged a nice picture of Eamonn Holmes I'd hoped to mount on card at a later date.*)

Oh, I've got a son called Darren
And a daughter whose name is Karen
Without them my life would be barren
Like living on the Isle of Arran

Toothbrush dilemmas

Before I begin discussing toothbrush dilemmas in earnest, there's a toothpaste dilemma we must solve. I realise that in many households (including my own) certain family members tend to discard perfectly usable tubes of toothpaste and open a fresh tube to replace it. Just because a tube of toothpaste looks empty doesn't mean it is! There may be several applications left in it, and it's incumbent on at least one family member to take matters into their own hands and rescue the prematurely discarded toothpaste from

Caught in the act! Although Kirsty has yet to commence scampering, her paw is placed mischievously over the TV Quick, suggesting fulliscale scampering is imminent!

the bathroom bin and give it a new lease of life. (If this means untangling it from a length of used dental floss, so be it.) However, as the 'rescued' toothpaste is not deemed acceptable for use by certain family members (like Mary!), the new toothpaste also must be kept in use, and hereby lies a dilemma:

How can you rescue the discarded toothpaste (and use it in tandem with the new one) but not have two toothpastes on the go?

The answer is: you can't. As with two tubs of margarine, two toothpastes on the go would be a nightmare scenario. So the rescued toothpaste must be kept hidden from the rest of the family and used secretly, which is what I do. It's quite exciting, actually. I'm currently using a tube of Macleans that I 'rescued' a fortnight ago, and I keep it in the medicine cabinet, hidden behind the calamine lotion. This is a safe hiding place as the lotion is in a large, heavy bottle, so it provides excellent shelter for the toothpaste, and it rarely gets used any more so prying eyes are unlikely to venture there and discover it.

John's Explanatory Note: It's a shame that the calamine lotion is so neglected. When I was a little lad it seemed to be in constant use, and stood proudly between a bag of cotton wool and a packet of lint. Still, it's reassuring to know it's still there, as a happy reminder of distant family summers.

I reckon another couple of squeezes from this toothpaste tube and I really will have to wave goodbye to it, and join the rest of the family in using the new one. That'll be a sad day, but then again, it won't be too long before that tube will be rejected by the others and I can claim it as my own, and the whole exciting and covert operation will begin again. But I digress...

Which is my toothbrush?

Whenever my wife Mary buys new toothbrushes for the family they are received with great excitement – by me, anyway. I don't think Darren gets that excited any more, and Karen certainly doesn't. In fact, now Karen lives away she no longer has a toothbrush in the rack, which is quite sad really. But any euphoria experienced at receiving a new toothbrush can swiftly turn to frustration and even anguish when you forget which colour brush is yours. Have you ever done that? I'm always doing it. And then when you go to brush your teeth you're faced with a dilemma: – which is your toothbrush? You NEED to know! After all, you don't want to use somebody else's! There's really nothing worse than using someone else's toothbrush (apart from having two margarines on the go? Yes, granted, or putting on Darren's underpants by accident, which I only did the once!).

So – what do you do if you can't remember which one is your toothbrush? Three simple tests will sort this matter out:

Test 1: Grasp the head of the toothbrush you think is yours. If it's wet then it can't be yours, can it, so you should go on to test 2. If it's dry you may think it's yours but before you assume that you must also carry out test 2. (And possibly test 3 too, but let's concentrate on test 2 first, shall we!)

Test 2: Grasp the heads of the other toothbrushes in the toothbrush holder, or beaker if that's how you store them (slightly insanitary, in my view, as the beaker collects a horrible grey residue. I don't know where that comes from – do you, readers?). Grasp each toothbrush head individually, and take your time – there's no rush. You've got to get this right! If any of those

241

toothbrushes have a wet head it means that they're probably not yours. They must have been recently used by the family member that owns that particular toothbrush. If they're all wet and the toothbrush in test 1 was dry, then that one must be yours, so go ahead and brush your teeth. Lucky you – you don't need to go on to test 3!

However, if the toothbrush you felt in test 1 was wet and one of the toothbrushes you grasped in test 2 was dry, then that dry one must be your toothbrush, and you just forgot which colour it was. But if more than one of them in test 2 was dry you have a problem, and if the toothbrush in test 1 was also dry you have even more of a dilemma! In all these cases you will need to go on to test 3.

Test 3: Line up the dry toothbrushes that you identified in test 2 (plus the test 1 toothbrush that you're pretty sure is yours because it was dry) and have a good hard look at them all.

Which one of them really is your toothbrush? Come on – think! If you don't know the answer then you may have to do 'Eeny meeny miny mo!' and risk using someone else's toothbrush, but in this situation, if you're really not sure, I'd suggest you just use the one that looks the cleanest and least used, which is a bit naughty, I suppose, but hopefully no one will be any be the wiser.

———————

John's Explanatory Note: Actual toothbrush ownership can be sorted out the following day during a family meeting, or by interviewing family members individually (in person preferably, but if that's not possible then by telephone, email or through the antisocial media platform now available to all!).

———————

TOOTHBRUSH TROUBLES

What if someone forgot which was their toothbrush and used yours by accident, meaning your toothbrush has a wet head? Won't the results of tests 1 and 2 be false and carrying out test 3 be pointless?

I'm afraid you're right! Someone else's memory might be as bad as yours and they've gone and used your toothbrush, thinking it was theirs. So when you grasped your toothbrush in test 1 and dismissed it as not being yours because it had a wet head, you shouldn't have done, because it WAS yours... oh, what a mess!

However, there's a little ray of sunshine here. If it's DAY 1 of new toothbrush ownership you can relax and even cut yourself a chuckle. Why? Well, if they were using the wrong toothbrush for the first time, you can simply do the same. Don't you see? You simply swap toothbrushes with no compromise of hygiene, and official change of ownership can be agreed at breakfast time.

But if only life were so simple. I'm now going to tell you a true story and cautionary tale that will make you think all this testing is a bit pointless, which I'm beginning to think it is, to be honest...

A cautionary toothbrush tale

One night a few years ago, several days after a completely new set of toothbrushes had been purchased from Superdrug by my wife Mary and distributed to all four family members, I mounted the stairs to brush my teeth prior to going to bed. Upon arriving at the bathroom, having spent a few minutes untangling the fringes of the bath mat which I noticed had become tangled, I reached for what I assumed was my toothbrush – the blue one. But then while routinely carrying out test 1 – disaster struck. "Oh no, it's already wet! What's going on?" I thought. "Am I mistaken and my toothbrush is actually NOT the blue one but the GREEN one?" (It definitely wasn't the purple or yellow one as they weren't my colour, and by doing test 2 I was able to verify this fact as the heads of those brushes were wet through).

I checked the green one for wetness and sure enough it was dry. Aha... so the green one was my toothbrush after all? I was blinking with disbelief because I could have sworn blind it was the blue one, but clearly I was wrong. My toothbrush must be the green one!

Then I whispered to meself, "No, no, no – it isn't! It is definitely the blue one!" Ooh blimey, I was starting to sweat. I wasn't panicking at that stage, readers, but, you know, it wasn't easy to remain calm. The thing is, I knew I HAD to keep calm to work out my next move!

John's Explanatory Note: If my old toothbrush (white with pink piping) had been there still, I could have used that one, but with cruel irony it had been removed from the holder that very afternoon and placed in the garage. I might at this stage have retrieved had it not already been placed in a jar of degreasing solvent and employed in cleaning a rusty lock I'd found abandoned round the back of the teaching hospital.

If it had been a reasonable hour a family meeting could have been called to verify toothbrush ownership and the dilemma averted. But it was 2.30 in the morning! I'd started watching watching *Judge John Deed* starring the charismatic Martin Shaw at midnight and fallen asleep on the sofa, and now, although I was wide awake, everyone in the house had gone to bed hours ago. Could I really justify waking them all to verify if the blue toothbrush was mine and tell off the culprit for using it accidentally? I carefully considered my options...

TOOTHBRUSH TROUBLES

Mary had gone to bed early with a headache and Karen, who was 15 at the time, had a GCSE exam in the morning. Neither would take kindly to being roused to ask which was their toothbrush, and tackling either of them would have been a very foolhardy action on my part. Besides, on reflection, neither Mary nor Karen would have chosen the wrong toothbrush. Theirs must be the purple and yellow ones, I decided.

My son Darren? Of course, he must be the culprit! Darren had been playing on his computer late that night after returning from working at Bargain Booze, so would have been distracted – in a reverie, still dwelling on the thrills of his video game. For him to absentmindedly select the wrong toothbrush would have been nothing out of the ordinary.

Then, before I could enter his bedroom to rouse Darren and give him a good telling-off, he appeared at the bathroom door.

"Ah Darren," I said, firmly but kindly. "You must have read my mind. Thank you for coming to see me to sort this matter out."

"You what, Dad?" he replied, in a baffled tone. "I've come to brush my teeth."

What??? I looked in amazement as Darren went straight to the toothbrush holder and without hesitation took the green toothbrush and brushed his teeth (having first primed the head with Ultrabrite). So the green toothbrush WAS Darren's, which explained why it had been dry. I retired to the landing, reeling from a new dilemma:

Who should be woken up first, wife or daughter, to ascertain which of them had used my blue toothbrush in error?

Before I could decide who, a memory suddenly popped into my head. Ken Worthington had called round earlier that evening to heat up his leftover curry in our microwave, as he often does, as previously stated. Anyway, on this occasion, as a dare, I'd tasted some of Ken's saggy bargey (is it really called that??). Oof, the flavour was almost as much of a shock to my taste buds as the first time I tried pestio (the green stuff that looks like mould in a jar – we discussed it earlier). My response had been to dash upstairs and… brush my teeth!

Of course, dear reader, you've worked it all out now, I trust? The blue toothbrush was MY toothbrush after all. I'd used it earlier, which is why the head was still wet, but I'd completely forgotten, and now I was left feeling like a complete idiot.

I went straight to bed and, although exhausted and emotionally drained, I lay awake for a long time looking at the ceiling, my heart racing, hoping that I wouldn't wake up Mary with my sighing. I was close to tears, realising I'd wasted a lot of time worrying about which toothbrush was mine. The worst thing was – I'd forgotten to brush my teeth! I really should have done because while I was watching TV earlier I'd devoured half a box of chocolate Brazil nuts! But I was too exhausted to get out of bed again.

So don't worry too much about which toothbrush is yours?

Maybe, I don't know any more. I don't think it's the most important domestic dilemma you'll come across in life. I also don't for one second think that Ken Worthington is ever in this boat, because – as I've stated many times throughout this book – Ken is a bachelor who lives alone, and there'll only ever be one toothbrush in his holder. Even if there were several, he could pick whichever one takes his fancy, safe in the knowledge that they're all his. He could even pretend the other toothbrushes belong to different imaginary people who live in the house with him, and so convince himself he's not alone in the world after all. Well, lucky old Ken!

"John? Who are you shouting at?" hisses Mary from outside the bathroom.

"Nobody, love," I reply, "I'm just finishing the chapter 'Toothbrush Troubles'."

"Oh I see. Well, hurry up – you've got a visitor!"

"Who, Mary?" I say with some consternation, having first unlocked the bathroom door so I can speak directly to my wife and establish eye contact with her. "Who's calling on us at such an anti-social hour?"

"Who do you think?" sighs Mary, before calling downstairs, "Ken? John will be down in a minute…"

Oof, Ken Worthington – I might have known. For a dreadful second I thought it might be the TV Licence Detection Team, but then I remembered our licence has a month and a half to run. How do I know that? I checked the renewal date only last week by logging in to my licence online (which you can do now, readers, it's a fantastic facility). Well, it would be but I couldn't remember the password and after three attempts was locked out of the account for twenty minutes. While waiting to be readmitted I thought about watching *The Chase*, but I was worried our licence might be invalid while I was locked out of the account, so I didn't. Instead I waited anxiously (crouched over Mary's laptop rubbing my hands together and occasionally stroking my chin, which I believe is normal behaviour when you're anxious) until I could try again, and then after two further unsuccessful attempts I decided to apply for a new password, which of course took a while to come through. By the time I finally got logged in to my licence and realised it was in date and closed down the laptop (that takes a while an' all – Mary needs to get a new one!), I turned on the TV to see the end credits of *The Chase* rolling and Bradley Walsh punching the air as he did a little shoe shuffle. It looked like I'd missed a cracker! Ah well…

"I'll be down in a second, Ken!" I call down the stairs before locking the bathroom door again and completing my ablutions.

I'm now squeezing hard on the toothpaste, but, oof… nothing's coming out! Now, I could go and get my pliers from the garage, which would surely help me extract the final traces of toothpaste from the tube, but I have a visitor and although it's only Ken, I need to urgently ascertain the reason for his arrival at such an ungodly hour. It hurts, but there's nothing for it − I must jettison this tube and use the other one.

CHAPTER 20:

HERE COMES MIDWEEK
(HOW TO ESCAPE DOMESTIC
DILEMMAS ENTIRELY!)

I'm sat now in the kitchen in my dressing gown with next-door neighbour (and sole agent) Ken Worthington who's perched on a bar stool enjoying a glass of our sherry that we bought in 2015 in Morrisons. As I've explained to Ken, we WERE saving that for next Christmas, but Ken's gleefully helped himself to a large schoonerful (plus a packet of Skips that I was going to have tomorrow while playing my organ). Ken insists he needed a drink to prepare himself to tell me something very important, so while he sips and munches away, I might as well collapse the ironing board. Oof, we forgot to discuss ironing-board dilemmas, but – thinking about it – there aren't any, are there? You just put the ironing board up when requested by your wife, and put it away again when she's finished with it.

"That's sexist, John!" Ken pipes up suddenly. "Why don't YOU ever do the ironing? It's not just a wife's duty, you know..."

"I know that, Ken," I respond swiftly, "and I DID do the ironing when Mary hurt her hand in 2009. But my chief role is to monitor Mary's progress – to ensure that the level in the water tank isn't getting too low, and to warn her if it looks like the hot iron is encroaching too closely to the flex. Anyway, this chapter isn't about dilemmas, although clearly there ARE ironing dilemmas after all, I was wrong, readers! Oh well, too late now. This chapter is to advise the readers of how to avoid domestic dilemmas in the first place. And it can be done. Do you know how, Ken?"

"Pour me another sherry and I'll have a guess," says Ken, cheekily.

"I'm afraid the answer's 'no', Ken, and if you don't mind me saying, you're treating our house as a late-night drinking den, and it's not on! Ooh, very well – have a small one. Oof, that's too much!"

"Thank you, John," chuckles Ken, refilling his schooner.

He takes another long noisy slurp of our sherry before saying, "I'm ready to tell you my important news now, John."

"That may be so, Ken, but first I have some rather important news myself that I must impart to the readers, as they've been waiting a good few paragraphs for this."

"Very well, John," replies Ken, huffily, shifting his position on our bar stool, while trying in vain to rest his Cuban heels on the cross-member.

Now, readers – the way to avoid domestic dilemmas entirely is simply to avoid a domestic environment entirely. In order to achieve that, you have to physically leave your home. Now, I don't mean you just hang around outside on the street because, well, that's tantamount to anti-social behaviour, isn't it? No, what I'm suggesting is doing something like borrowing Doreen Melody's camper van and embarking on a mini break. (I'm not sure she'll be lending it us for a while, however – not after today's shenanigans.) In order to get ourselves into the mood for a mini break, I suggest we sing another of my songs, but softly, please, as it's late, and I don't want the sound to carry upstairs and disturb Mary.

"Should the camper van have a sturdy chrome ladder giving direct access to the roof?" enquires Ken, dreamily.

"In an ideal world, Ken, yes it should. So let's begin the number, and do join in when you feel confident."

"I will indeed, John. Thank you!"

CARAVAN CAPERS

The houseplants have been watered
We've cancelled the milk and papers
If anyone calls, say we're on our hols
Indulging in caravan capers

We've bolted the doors and windows
Bid farewell to neighbours
It's time to take a well-earned break
and embark on caravan capers

Oh, how long will it take us?
What rural thrills await us?
I long to be at the water tap
Enjoying banter with a fellow camper

Caravan capers! Caravan capers!

The campsite sounds amazing
The facilities are wide-ranging
Although we may throughout our stay
Be surrounded by animals grazing

With baaing lambs to wake us
How happy our stay will make us
A leisurely groom in the gents' washroom
And then a hearty full English breakfast

Caravan capers! Caravan capers!

Oh, how long will it take us?
What rural thrills await us?
I long to be at the water tap
Enjoying banter with a fellow camper

Caravan capers! Caravan capers!

"Ah, happy days… Although you were rather shrill there, Ken, if you don't mind me saying."

"I was enjoying myself, John, as one should on a mini break!"

It doesn't have to be a mini break, of course – it could be just a day trip. The Pencil Museum in Keswick is a bit far away though, would you not say, for a day trip? And a journey to the caverns near Castleton may be too much for an old car like my Austin Ambassador (the Winnats Pass is one in three, you know!). Besides, you can get white stuff on your cagoule after accidental contact with the ancient rock.

Oof, perhaps it's better to stay at home after all and accept those domestic dilemmas as and when they come to us. At least now – armed with all the useful advice given in this book, you'll be fully equipped to deal with any crisis (mini or full-blown), and I wish you every success in your future life, readers, whatever there is remaining of it, and erm, nobody knows what that is, which is slightly annoying, in my view. How can we plan a final trip to check the level of the reservoir, if we don't know that it's the final trip? Ooh, life's frustrating, isn't it?

Keen rock climbers may be aghast at my unsuitable footwear and lack of shackle and harness. Did I really scale that cliff without them? No, I didn't! To the left of those rocks is a gentle grassy slope, and I strolled up it in a leisurely fashion!

"You're forgetting one thing, John!" Ken announces, grandly.

"Really, Ken? And what might that be?"

"You should treat EVERY trip to the reservoir as your last, John, and so should the readers," explains Ken, with a philosophical smile. "That way, you're going to really enjoy it!"

"Brilliant, Ken!" I say, impressed by Ken's clever thinking. But then I realise Ken's argument is fundamentally flawed, and so I continue, gravely, "But, Ken − what if the ice cream van isn't there? You're going to feel devastated, and cheated to some degree. Worrying about the prospect of never having another ice cream means you won't be able to fully enjoy checking the level of the reservoir!"

"Ooh, yes, you're right, John," Ken admits, sheepishly. "I hadn't thought of that."

"No, you didn't think it through, Ken, as − if you don't mind me saying − you so often don't! May I suggest you strike out your foolish idea when you do the proofreading?"

"Well, actually, John," says Ken, slowly, as he puts down his schooner on our worktop, "erm… I've decided not to strike out anything. I've decided your book doesn't need to be proofread, after all."

"What! Really, Ken? Do you mean it?" I ask, incredulously. "That's terrific news!"

"Yes, I think your book should be published as it is − warts and all."

"Excuse me, there's no warts in this book, Ken," I reply, gruffly, "and there's no rude bits either, so please don't think about inserting any. Well no, you've just agreed not to, and I thank you for that. Yes, thanks, Ken − I appreciate your not censoring me, and giving me free artistic rein."

"As I would any of my artistes," Ken replies, breezily. "When Julie Satan told me she wanted to go on stage wearing a basque and a leather gauntlet while wielding a broadsword, I was initially dubious, but I said nothing, and I was justified in my decision. She now has a bi-monthly residency at the Birley Moor Ex-Servicemen's Institute. So, why don't we celebrate my decision by having a little singsong?"

"We've just had one, Ken, and your crooning may have disturbed my wife as she applies her cold cream," I reply, adding warily, "What song do you suggest?"

"'Up And Down Like A Bride's Nightie'?"

"No, Ken, that song is too blue for this book. Despite what you just said, you're trying to turn this book into a bonkbuster after all!"

"You're wrong, John! That song is a sensitive and insightful exploration into the phenomenon of mood swings!" insists Ken, before breaking into song.

I'm up and down like a bride's nightie
Up and down and I don't know why, ee oo...
I'm happy and then I'm blue!

I notice Ken has turned crimson – the result of singing a risqué number unaccompanied? Perhaps, but also because Ken is incapable, as he has been since he was on *New Faces* in 1973, of sustaining a solo performance in either a public or a private arena. What a tragedy!

"All right then," says Ken, more soberly. "What do you suggest we sing, because it's been a long day with many ups and downs, and I need a nice number to send me off home?"

"'Eggs And Gammon'?" I reply, mischievously. "Eggs and gammon, poor Rhiannon, Ken had wind! Oof Ken, what's the matter?" (I add, noticing that Ken has fallen silent.)

"It's not kind to remind me of that very sad time, John, when I was stuck in a tent with a poorly tummy. That was the last holiday I ever spent with Rhiannon," muses Ken, sadly.

"I realise it's painful for you, Ken. I just thought that because it's a bit childish and contains lavatorial humour, the publishers might like it and be able to market the book to a broader cross-range of punters?" I teasingly suggest to Ken.

"Mm, interesting!" says Ken, cocking his head to one side. "But if you don't mind, I'd prefer to sing this number…"

Ken clears his throat and – despite going very red again – begins to sing one of my classic rock anthems, which celebrates the perfect venue for a day trip, with no chance of domestic dilemmas, although it could turn you against jaspers (wasps, remember?) and it shouldn't really, as they're very important pollinators, so I've heard.

DANDELION AND BURDOCK

Looking back to a better time
When life was good and there was little crime
Children played on their pogo sticks
And on Saturday went to the local flicks
And we all drank big bottles of pop
Especially dandelion and burdock
What I'd give for a tiny slurp
Though it stung your nose and it made you burp

We were always polite to bobbies
On Remembrance Day
We all wore poppies
And we all had useful hobbies

At the Crich Tram Museum
I was with a friend called Ian
We were there from nine
Till chucking-out time
There was so much there worth seeing
At the Crich Tram Museum

Disaster befell poor Ian
A vicious jasper made him drop
His dandelion and burdock
Oh, that jasper made him drop
His dandelion and burdock

Ian's bottle had developed a crack
So he couldn't get his deposit back
Tuppence may not seem a lot
But it would buy you a big fat lollipop
Blackjacks were ten a penny
Remember now I'm talking old money
Not that we ever had any

(But we were happy. Well, I was…)

Cycling with my peers
The wind whistling past my ears
As we reached Mam Tor
I was grateful for
My Sturmey Archer gears

At the Crich Tram Museum
I was with a friend called Ian
We were there from nine
Till chucking-out time
There was so much there worth seeing
At the Crich Tram Museum
Disaster befell poor Ian
A vicious jasper made him drop
His dandelion and burdock

Oh, that jasper made him drop
His dandelion and burdock
Oh, but how I'd love a drop
Of dandelion and burdock!

Mmm, I wouldn't mind a glass of pop right now, but I've just brushed my teeth. Oof, Ken's begun singing again. I knew I shouldn't have let him have that second sherry! He's now singing 'Here Comes Midweek', which is highly apt, however, as midweek is almost upon us. And somehow, although domestic dilemmas DO occur in the middle of the week, they never seem as fraught with misery as those that happen at the weekend. Oof, Ken's coming up to the chorus. I think we'd better join in, don't you, readers?

HERE COMES MIDWEEK

Here comes midweek!
I'm so excited I can hardly speak
But I've got to, to tell you
Here comes midweek!
Strap on your bumbags and stride into the street
And we'll be having fun till Thursday evening comes

It's midweek and we are free
To renew our books at the library
Have '2 for 1' deals at the carvery
Go on – be a devil
Let's go to the reservoir... and check the level!

"What a lovely idea, John. Let's do that right now!" says Ken, clambering off the bar stool. "And we don't have to imagine it's our last trip there, because I'm sure it won't be."

"Unless the ice cream van's there, in which case it doesn't matter if it's our final trip – we'll die happy!"

"Yes we will! Let's go!"

"Hang on... you're being silly, Ken. It's pitch black out there. We'll go late morning and take a flask and a couple of Rocky Bars."

"Oh you will, will you?" says Mary sternly, suddenly appearing at the kitchen door with her hands on her hips. "Well, you'd better get some sleep then. And I wouldn't mind getting some myself, now... GOODNIGHT!!"

And with that Mary closes the door, rather firmly, actually, suggesting she doesn't approve of our little late-night singsong. It's been a very long day – for all of us, and it's time now for next-door neighbour and sole agent Ken Worthington to quit the premises and exit our lives... for ever! No, that would be a bit harsh. Although sometimes Ken does get on my nerves, I'd miss him dreadfully.

As Ken does up his leather jacket (the one that looks a bit like the one Lovejoy used to wear) there's just time for a final (whispered) reprise of the chorus...

Here comes midweek!
I'm so excited I can hardly speak
But I've got to, to tell you
Here comes midweek!
Strap on your bumbags and stride into the street
And we'll be having fun
Yes, we'll be having fun
We'll be having fun till Thursday evening comes
Here comes midweek!

CHAPTER 21:

BED ROOM AND TICKS

If Ken Worthington had decided to proofread this chapter he'd have been rubbing his hands with glee. Why? Well, read the title out loud, readers. What does it sound like when you say it? It sounds like something else, doesn't it? Something a bit cheeky, and Ken would surely have had no hesitation in changing the title to 'Bedroom Antics' so he could promote this book as a steamy bonkbuster after all! That'd have been a shame because 'Bed Room and Ticks' is a much better title. You see, fitting a bed into a bedroom so there's both room for a bedside cabinet AND easy access to your side of the bed is often a dilemma. Do you have no cabinet meaning your water beaker must be placed directly on the floor allowing a daddy longlegs to climb into it, or do you have the cabinet but forgo access to your side of the bed – forcing you to clamber over your partner, risking squashing them and thereby receiving a tirade of abuse? Moreover, you DO get ticks and dust mites in the bed sometimes and that's a dilemma, an' all. Also, you get the annoying 'tick' of clocks in the bedroom, which can be a blinking nuisance. The very clever and apt title 'Bed Room and

Ticks' means I can discuss ALL these dilemmas in the same chapter. So anyone hoping to find anything in this chapter of a saucy nature – forget it, my friend!

Duvet or blanket, quilt or counterpane?

Obviously, there is no dilemma here because everyone has a duvet these days, don't they? (I'm under mine right now, in my pyjamas and sitting up in bed waiting for Mary, who has decided to go to the bathroom to weigh herself.) But historically 'choice of bedding' was a huge dilemma, which had a massive impact on the nation, and to pretend it didn't happen would be irresponsible. As I recall, thirty-five years ago when duvets (formerly known as the continental quilt) came in there was a bit of a national crisis. Should we stick with traditional bedding or take a chance on the new-fangled duvet, which seemed like it wouldn't work, because it didn't tuck you in around the edges? So how on earth could you get to sleep with a big draught blowing in at the sides?

John's Explanatory Note: Some of the younger readers may be laughing at me now, but that's fine – go ahead and laugh! Older readers may be laughing too, but it will only be because they're being tickled or perhaps something funny is going on outside in the street, not because of the fears we once all had about duvets, because they were very real!

When I was a lad I often used to help my mum make the beds, and it went like this: bottom sheet first (you see, that's not changed, younger readers... You've stopped your laughing now, I'm glad to see), then another sheet, upon which was placed one or two, sometimes three blankets, all of which had to be tucked in under the mattress – nice and tightly, if you please. Then came the eiderdown, which often had an exotic pattern on it comprised of swirling roses, very well drawn by an artist the world has long forgotten. You might think that was it, but no – on top of the eiderdown you placed a counterpane, which was like a big cloak for the bed and held everything in place.

Come bedtime you had to get in under all that lot and although the sheer weight of it made you feel very safe and snug, unfortunately you had to lie on your side at all times. You couldn't lie on your back or your feet would get crushed and misshapen by half a hundredweight of bedding bearing down on you. I suppose we could have untucked the sheet and blankets to relieve the pressure, but we never did because we were worried about (A) being told off, (B) a terrible draught whistling up under the covers and freezing your toes off, plus torso and other limbs.

Aha… if only we'd known that doing that would have just transformed the bedding into an early duvet and that air pockets would have formed all around, creating a barrier and preventing the cold from entering. If we'd known that we would have slept easily in our beds – yes, well, we would have, quite literally! In fact, thinking about it makes me feel a bit angry, and really old people should be livid because they spent so many years lying on their sides at night, or if they didn't, having their toes bent. None of this need have happened if only Monsieur Duvet (I presume he's French?) could have got his product on the market a little bit sooner!

Anyway, he has now, and it's lovely, in't it – the duvet? Absolutely smashing, and I can't think of anything else to say about duvets. Except: I prefer the term 'continental quilt' and would gladly spearhead a campaign to reinstate it, except I don't have the time, sorry. You're welcome to do it though, if you can be bothered…

Duvet covers

Oof, don't get me started on them – they're a right nuisance, aren't they? Correctly aligning the poppers or buttons on a double or king-size duvet is one of the trickiest jobs for members of the public. It really is, and thinking about it, doesn't that cancel out all the advantages of having a lightweight covering that doesn't cripple yer toes? In other words, shouldn't we abandon the duvet and go back to blankets, eiderdown and counterpane, knowing that we don't have to tuck them in? Oof, probably not, but it's a bit of a dilemma after all, isn't it, readers?

John's Explanatory Note: Mary and I have a double duvet, to go with our double bed, but I've heard a lot of young couples nowadays are plumping for a king-size duvet (and king-size bed!). This to me seems very presumptuous: unless you're really a king you should stick with the double, like we've always done.

Why can't we dispense with the duvet cover and just use the duvet?

Well, we could I suppose, but my wife would have a fit, understandably. Hygiene issues aside, scuff marks and even footprints might appear on the duvet, and it would need washing on a weekly basis, and they're so big they're a devil to even get in the machine. Oof no, we need to retain the duvet cover – they just need to invent a better system for sealing the cover around the duvet. Aha – it exists, of course: – Velcro! I mentioned earlier how much I enjoy the ripping sound it makes when the nurse takes your blood pressure thingy off your arm, but you know, it wasn't always so. As a younger man, I used to find the sound of Velcro being pulled apart rather disquieting, as this little ditty demonstrates:

THE SWISH OF CAGOULE

The swish of cagoule
Boy, it makes me drool
The zup of a zip
Does the trick
The flap of a tent
Brings me merriment
But the crunch of Velcro
Makes me sick!

Bed bugs bug, and mites might mightily!

That's a very clever subtitle, if I don't mind saying so myself. However, I've realised I'm not really qualified to talk about dust mites and bed ticks, and all that. If you have a problem with them I suggest you ring up the council and speak to the environmental health officer, or just Google it like I'm about to.

Well... I never knew that! Apparently: 'bed bugs are insects (they have 6 legs), whereas ticks are arachnids (like spiders – with 8 legs). Bed bugs feed mainly on human blood but can bite animals, whereas ticks prefer animal blood but will bite humans if cornered.'

Ugh, that's awful! But it's good to know what we're dealing with, in't it, readers? And there's a bit more: 'Bed bugs and ticks can't jump or fly, so they hitch rides on people, pets, and objects to travel long distances. People and pets usually pick up ticks while walking in tall grass or other tick habitats.' (That's why you need to cut the grass – reread Chapter 15: THE LAWN NEEDS

MOWING, BUT I NEED A NAP!) On the other hand: 'Bed bugs often attach themselves to luggage at infested hotels or hide inside second-hand furniture.'

Do they now? They're obviously quite intelligent creatures knowingly getting free holidays like that. But why are they hiding? They must realise that they shouldn't be there. And why do they not hide in new furniture? A psychiatrist might argue it's because they suffer from low self-esteem and feel unworthy to travel in a brand new wardrobe. I personally would argue all it shows is this: being brainy isn't necessarily going to lead to a contented life. Enough about bugs. What about:

Annoying ticking clocks in the bedroom

The dilemma here is that often two people can disagree about whether a clock's tick is comforting or annoying. I bought a lovely little fold-up travel alarm clock from a jumble sale in 2004 for 10p. Before you say, "Blimey, 10p? That cheap!", let me tell you that when I bought it, it didn't work, the battery compartment cover was missing, and it was absolutely filthy and caked in a strange rubbery substance that took me an hour to scrape off with a Stanley knife. Suddenly 10p sounds a bit pricey, doesn't it?

Anyhow, I fell in love with the tick, once I'd cleaned the badly rusted battery terminals, put a battery in – sealing the compartment with a strip of duct tape – and got the thing going. It was loud, yes, but reassuringly regular (mind you, you expect that in a clock really, don't you?).

However, during the first night of usage, Mary decided that she didn't like it. It was keeping her awake, she alleges. I was in the land of Nod, having been lulled to sleep by the soothing tick of my new clock, and I had to be roughly roused by Mary. I was in no mood to hear the news that she didn't like the clock's tick and I must take the battery out. I did so, but I was extremely unhappy about it, because I then had to lie listening to Mary's breathing (no barking fox that night, thankfully. Instead, a strange sound as if she was being throttled – a little phlegm in Mary's throat perhaps?).

But with no reassuring tick to listen to I couldn't get back to sleep, and I found myself just staring at the alarm clock's little luminous hands, knowing full well that there was no point really because they weren't moving, and that the time was wrong, and getting more wrong with every tick it was missing. I felt so sad and empty, it was almost as if time was standing still for me. "Ooh," you could argue, "in that case the clock was accurately reflecting the time for you, and so was still a working instrument. Putting the battery back in would have only made the time wrong!" I see where you're coming from but no, my friend... if it was working again I'd have become happy and so time wouldn't have been standing still for me any more. "Ooh," you could then argue, "does that mean it doesn't matter if a clock you're fond of is working or not because it's ALWAYS going to be accurately reflecting the time you feel it is?" Um, I don't know... Look, we don't have any more time to discuss this argument about Time – it's silly!

Although sadly decommissioned, my little alarm clock remained for several years in the bedroom sitting on top of my bedside book, a war novel by Len Deighton that took me six years to read! Well, I kept forgetting what had happened in the previous chapter, and so had to recap in order to progress with the story, but by the time I'd read a couple of pages of the previous chapter, I was out for the count.

———

John's Explanatory Note: The recapping became so regular and extensive that at one point I realised I was actually going backwards! At that stage, I seriously considered reading the last chapter first to see if I might make more progress that way. It was probably a silly idea, which I never implemented. And I never did finish the book, eventually donating it to the Sue Ryder charity shop, where it remains to this day. Now and again when I'm in there looking for a knick-knack, I take it off the shelf to check the pages for evidence of yellowing, but I never bother trying to pick up the story. Far too complicated, Len, if you're reading this!

———————————

Back to the clock. I also used it as a paperweight to secure petrol receipts and a napkin that had come from a Little Chef in 2007 which – being unused and unsoiled – I kept by my bedside as a 'relief tissue' with which to blow my nose if my normal supply of Handy Andies wasn't to hand. But before that could happen, Mary threw the napkin away, claiming it was soiled. It wasn't – it was just a bit dusty, and the Little Chef logo had faded badly due to repeated sunlight exposure. (Yes, our bedroom window is south facing – well spotted, readers!) If only the clock had been positioned immediately over the logo, it wouldn't have faded. You think about these things when it's too late. Somehow, losing the napkin, and realising that the clock had failed to keep the napkin logo from fading, made me fall out of love with it, and one day I... well, I chucked it away. I'm sorry, clock...

Foam or feather?

This will get people foaming at the mouth, and indeed, the feathers flying! Nothing causes more rancour in a bedroom than arguments about pillows and whether the filling of someone's allocated pillow will prevent them getting a good sleep that night. Oh yes, pillow dissatisfaction is extremely high on the list of things couples argue about, I'm sure it is. I don't know why you never see it mentioned when they do those surveys about reasons for divorce. I'm sure it's only because nobody's asked the question! It's always 'putting furniture together' that causes marital breakdown, if you believe the surveys. Utter rubbish, in my view. Mary and I never put furniture together together, or take it apart apart, for that matter. No, we buy it ready assembled, thank you, after trying it out in the Furniture Village showroom. If our furniture was ever in pieces we'd be asking for a full refund!

Foam or feather: – it's up to you. Mary and I have foam nowadays – more hygienic and kinder to our feathered friends, says our Karen, although feather pillows make for more dramatic pillow fights, I suppose! (If they burst!)

If a pillow label is tickling you, should you leave it be?

This is a funny one, isn't it? It's just popped into my head, and the correct answer to the dilemma is, no – you simply remove the pillow from the pillowslip and then reinsert the pillow the other way so the labels are safely hidden inside the pillowslip, and unable to tickle you.

But one weekend a good few years ago, we stayed at the house of my brother-in-law Carl and his wife, Susan who used to work in finance but she doesn't any more, and what she did exactly I've no idea so there's no point in dwelling on it, so let's move on with my story, if we may… Mary and I were sleeping in their spare room, because next day we were all attending a family funeral near Milton Keynes. Whether or not there was quiche afterwards I don't recall, and like Susan's job I'd rather not go into it because the important thing is this: As I was nodding off, I realised Mary wasn't settling at all. She seemed to be swatting something with her hand and tutting. Then her light went on and I felt the pillow under my head being prodded. What on earth was going on?

"Oof, what ARE you doing, Mary!" I barked forcibly, though she took no notice and carried on pulling at the pillow.

"Your pillow labels are scratching me, John," replied Mary, in a quiet but determined tone, "so they're coming... OFF!"

And as she said the last word I heard a terrible ripping sound as she tore off the main label of the poor pillow. I was aghast.

"What the hell have you done, Mary?" I whispered hoarsely. "You've broken the pillow!"

"No I haven't," retorted Mary, snorting slightly. "This one's coming off, an' all!"

And with that there was another awful sound of cloth being ripped asunder as Mary tore off the pillow's smaller subsidiary label (containing washing, dry cleaning and other pillow-care information). Had Mary gone mad? I sat up in bed and looked at my wife, who was now calmly lying back on her pillow with a satisfied smile on her face, and two pillow labels held in her clenched fist. I took them from her and gazed at them, shell-shocked. Was this the same woman I'd married? Never in all our years together had I witnessed her do something as crazy as that. Such was the violence of her actions, it reminded me of a head being ripped off a chicken, or something horrible like that. Had Mary secretly joined the Hells Angels? Isn't that what they do for the initiation ceremony? Ken told me that once.

Mary gave a satisfied snort and rolled over and went back to sleep, but get this: with her head pointing the other way, so she was miles away from where she claimed the labels had been scratching her face. Why hadn't she just turned round before, instead of attacking my pillow labels? Unbelievable! Anyway, she told me to switch the light out, but I didn't. How could I sleep now? I was wide awake. I just lay holding these labels, which the manufacturer had attached to the pillow for a very good reason – to advise the pillow user of how to use the pillow and best care for it. Look at this way, readers: would you rip up the operating manual for a new combi boiler? No, you wouldn't. But what Mary had done was akin to that. I lay wondering what Carl and his wife Susan would think when they discovered the grisly truth? I suppose the labels could be stitched back on, so yes, Mary would have to do that, but not now – in the morning.

Before I turned off the light I studied the labels, and I have to say, they made for interesting bedtime reading. Within a few minutes I had learnt what '65% cotton' is in twenty different languages (don't ask me to remember now though!), oh yes, and '35% mod acrylic lining'. Fascinating stuff! I even learnt that a pillow's size is 50 by 80 centimetres or 20 by 32 inches. Did you know that, readers? Well, you do now! Eventually I fell asleep clutching my new night-time book, but incredibly, next morning Carl and Susan didn't seem that bothered when I told them what Mary had done. They were even laughing about it – a reaction that saddened me. Indeed, as we left, Carl popped his hand through my car window and offered me the two labels, saying "Haven't you forgotten something, John?" I realise he was trying to be funny, but I didn't find it remotely amusing, so I ignored him and kept reversing out of their drive.

John's Explanatory Note: I wish I'd taken the labels off him now as they'd have sat nicely in my glasses case, and should I ever have mislaid my cleaning cloth, they would have done the job just fine, keeping my specs sparkling and dust- and grime-free. Although maybe not, as they WERE a bit scratchy and might have damaged the lenses.

I think that's it for bedroom dilemmas. Apart from sleeping there's nothing much else that goes on in a bedroom, is there? I'm not going to tackle odd socks in the sock drawer. It's up to you to put some time aside to pair them up, as I've already stated. "Ooh, hello Mary!"

"You're STILL talking to yourself!" says Mary, walking in from the bathroom, tutting. "You'd better not be doing this tomorrow, John, cos you've driven me crackers today!"

"I know I have, Mary, and I apologise," I reply, getting up off the bed. "And Ken and Joan – I've upset them too. And I'm very sorry about that, but I'm glad everyone's friends again."

"Oh yes, everything will be just fine," says Mary, sniffing determinedly, before climbing into bed.

"Oh good," I reply, feeling relief that the day's ending with me and Mary getting on well again. "The book's very nearly finished now, Mary, and tomorrow, you'll be pleased to learn, I'm writing a song for Leo Sayer, or maybe Coldplay, so I'll be in the garage on my organ and out of your way."

"Oh good. Well, please stop prattling on now because I want to read my book, if you don't mind."

"That's fine, Mary – I won't say a word," I say, and then I fall silent.

Oof, Mary may want to read her book, but what about me? I've got a book to finish writing, which is far more important! By the way, readers, although I'm carrying on, I'm not talking. This bit and what follows is being typed into my tablet (ooh, that reminds me, I need to take my tablets, excuse me...)

Right, I'm back again. Erm, as I was saying, although I'm not talking, I'm typing on an electronic device, so you're still able to access my thoughts. Clever, isn't it?

This will be me tomorrow, readers — playing my organ in my garage. But I won't wear a silly expression like this — I'll be frowning with my head down as I hone some lyrics for little Leo…

John's Explanatory Note: Some may argue it's not that clever, and most books are written this way. But frankly, I don't have the time or the patience to be typing away all night. I'm only doing it now so as not to annoy Mary, but it's ever so slow, as my fingers are too big for the little buttons, and I keep on typing in the wrong worm... sorry, word!

We'll end this chapter (and the book) discussing – if we may – my son Darren's cabin bed. He had had it for years, since he was a little lad, and couldn't bear to part with it, even when he was a lanky teenager and his feet were poking out at the end. I think he felt safe in it, and I understand that because one night I slept in it after me and Mary had had a bad row (which happens very rarely, I do assure you!). Darren was staying at a friend's house so the bed was free. Once I'd been given my marching orders, instead of going down into the lounge to kip on the sofa, I remembered there was a child's sleeping bag in the loft that had khaki markings on it. So I got it down and climbed up into Darren's cabin bed. Well, the sleeping bag was ever so tight, and the bed was cramped and wobbling a bit every time I shifted my position, but in a way that added to the excitement. The military markings on my sleeping bag made it easy to imagine I was a soldier bedded down in cramped conditions prior to commencing a dangerous manoeuvre the following morning, which, in a way – trying to patch things up with Mary – I was going to be!

One day, the cabin bed collapsed. It was an accident waiting to happen as Darren was way too heavy for it (and I suppose my night of being a soldier in it didn't help!) and all the planks fell through the base, so then he had to sleep on the floor. But Darren wasn't remotely fazed by his sudden change in sleeping arrangements. For a long time he'd been asking if he could sleep on just a double mattress, you know, straight on the floor without a base. Apparently, another student at his college was doing it and he was encouraging Darren to do the same. I wasn't happy about it initially as it's a bit like what a hippy would do, isn't it, in a commune, do you not think? Mary wasn't concerned but I was worried it might lead to drug taking, or tarot card reading, strange activities like that.

Anyway, we let Darren do that, buying him a double mattress – once we'd sold the cabin bed – but my fears appeared to be justified when he swapped his warm white light bulb for a red one, and then one night I smelt the aroma of a joss stick wafting from his room. (I found the packet later with some funny symbols printed on it, plus a drawing of a lady with too many arms.) My other concern was that, being so low down, Darren wouldn't be able to access his bedside cabinet properly. But I needn't have worried – he got rid of that, an' all! All he had by his bed was a big box of tissues, and he was getting through a lot of them. And I know exactly why that was! Well, lying close to the floor as Darren was, he was caught in a permanent draught so he was always catching a cold, and so needed to constantly blow his nose.

Darren's off the floor now – he's got a proper bed again with a hygienic pine frame, and perhaps he'll take it with him when he eventually leaves our house and sets up a home with a young wife and they start a family, like me and Mary did all those years ago. I'm not sure when that'll be as Darren spends far too long playing his computer games to have time to do much courting. In fact, it's a long while since he's brought a lass home to meet us. A few years ago he was seeing a stocky lass called Jasmine who played the cornet in a local youth orchestra. I liked her and she'd have made a good wife for Darren. It's a shame it didn't work out. She could have stood next to the bed and blasted out a tune on the cornet each morning to rouse him. He likes his bed, does Darren!

And our Karen's taking a while to find a fella, it seems. Her and her flatmate Maxine have just announced they're going to get a dog from a rescue centre which, though laudable, ties Karen down a bit and makes it difficult for her to go out dancing on the spur of the moment, or for a spin in a sports car, should she get an invite from a prospective suitor. Well, you never know!

———————

John's Explanatory Note: I've just remembered that as well as a proper bed, Darren once again has a bedside cabinet, with a lamp that boasts a digital light bulb that changes colours every few seconds, which is very clever. I'd quite like one like that in our room but I don't think Mary's that keen.

———————

"You're not that keen, are you, Mary, on having a light like our Darren's got?" I say to Mary out loud, deciding that I've been thinking and typing for long enough.

But Mary doesn't reply. She must be concentrating on her book. But hang on, oof… it looks like she's nodded off without reading a single page of her book on essential oils that Joan Chitty got her for Christmas.

When Mary and I were courting I used to sing to her 'The Happy Wanderer' while we were out walking in our cagoules near Froggatt Edge, but that's not suitable for bedtime really as it has that loud high bit – "Falda Dee, Falda Dah, Falda Dee, Falda Dah Dah Dah Dah!", which used to make Mary laugh. It is comically high I suppose, close to the vocal range of that lad from The Rubettes. What happened to them then – they've gone very quiet? Good, I say, because his voice could give you a headache!

The song I'm going to end with is much more soothing, and was inspired by the experience of trying to sell Darren's cabin bed, which we did, once I'd repaired it. It should be performed by one gentleman and one lady, ideally dressed in Victorian apparel, so should I wake Mary and ask her to sing the lady's part? Er no, I think I've upset my wife enough for one day. But it IS a duet, and I could teach her the lady's part quite easily. Oof, it's a dilemma. But haven't we had enough dilemmas for one day? Yes, we have. Look, it's not a problem – I'll take both parts, but just so you know who's who, the lady's lines will be in italics.

CABIN BED

Oh, who will buy my cabin bed?
To tell the truth, it's my son's
And in a way to me that bed
Will always be Darren's
But now it is too small for him
The end plank chafes his ankles
Oh who will buy my cabin bed?
Buyer to dismantle.

I'm interested in your cabin bed
And would like a quick perusal
Well thank you, madam, but another
Mum has first refusal
I'll leave a contact number
And should the sale fall through
Please give me a tinkle
And let my dream come true

Cabin bed, cabin bed!
It's made of black ash
Cabin bed, cabin bed!

276

BED ROOM AND TICKS

It's had a slight bash
Cabin bed, cabin bed!
Though I'd prefer cash
I suppose a cheque will do

Tell me more of your cabin bed
How long has it been here?
The boy was ten when the purchase was made
He's nineteen now, so nine years
Where will your son sleep now?
Is his new bed an improvement?
Well no, it's a mattress on the floor
He's just like a flippin' student

Oh this cabin bed seems so cosy and warm
Yes, and if I was smaller I'd make it my own

For the sweetest dreams are to be had
By anyone who lies here
And the Ninja Turtle stickers?
They're included in the price, dear
I must admit I'm tempted
I'll sleep on it, if I may
No, you're too big, it's designed for a kid
Oh what a thing to say!

And yet it could be lengthened
To fit an adult male
I'm sorry, but I've changed my mind
This cabin bed is not for sale!

"Light, John…" murmurs Mary, but kindly, with no hint of anger, which is nice of her, because I was starting to sing quite stridently towards the end.

277

"Yes love, sorry to wake you up. I'm all done now, by the way. The book is FINALLY finished!"

"Oh good. Sleep tight…"

"Goodnight, love. Thank you for being my wife, Mary," I say, as I line up an emergency Rennie, so as not to disturb her during the night. My water beaker is positioned not too close to my bedroom light, or to the edge of my bedside cabinet. I have a little practice reaching out for it in the dark by closing my eyes and feeling for it.

John's Explanatory Note: I recommend you do the same thing, readers, if you're in my position – in bed at night-time, and about to switch the light off. Oh, and I do hope you've enjoyed the explanatory notes I've provided throughout the book. This is the last one, by the way!

"Light, John!" Mary murmurs, but a bit louder this time, and with the hint of a snarl in her voice!

"Oof!" I whisper. "Good night, readers!"

Sorry, I couldn't find a photo of me in my pyjamas, so here's another one of me reading the TV Quick. Although I'm still not really reading it, am I? That week's issue can't have been very interesting, can it...

ACKNOWLEDGEMENTS

I would like to thank my mother, Joan Fellows, for giving birth to me, and Chris Phipps, Martin Willis, Paul Jenkins, Phillip Hall, John Heywood and my father, Derek Fellows, for helping me in various ways to give birth to John Shuttleworth. I can't thank any of them in person, however, for sadly they have all died. Still alive – at least as I write – is the real Ken Worthington: my sole agent Richard Bucknall of RBM management whom I thank for his unwavering support over the last twenty-eight years; thank you to David Barraclough of Omnibus Press for commissioning this book and for his ever-cheerful encouragement, to Catherine Best for shrewd copy-editing and to Imogen Gordon Clark for her patience and excellent advice during the book editing process; thanks to Alice, Suzie, George and Paddy for being my kids, and to Lorna, Sally and Clare for being my sisters; to Miriam Holland – thanks for being my girlfriend and helping me obtain wood whenever the fires of inspiration needed replenishing; for professional advice over the years I thank my wonderful radio show producer Dawn Ellis, and the man who brought John Shuttleworth to Radio 4 – Paul Schlesinger; also thanks to Andrew Shilcock for tirelessly running the John Shuttleworth Appreciation Society online shop, and for setting up and running the John Shuttleworth website (www. shuttleworths.co.uk), thanks to Joe Margetts for establishing John's

Twitter page (@johnshuttlewrth) and brilliantly masquerading as John for several years before I stepped in and took over; a big thanks too for various reasons to Willy Smax, Will Yapp, Martin Parr, Keith Morrison, Faye, Karel Beer, Steve Lindsey, Elly Spilberg, Lorraine Bowen, Steve Pagett, Kevin Baldwin, Chris Sidwell, Rosy Clayton, Alan Clift, Tony Briggs, Richard Lake, Alan Mumby, Matt Strathern, Robert Anderson; and finally... to anyone I have bumped into during the last thirty-five years who has (however unwittingly) given me an idea (however slim) that ended up as a John Shuttleworth observation or a song... you might not know who you are and I can't remember anyway which is just as well because I may owe you a royalty... but you'll have to make do with the final thank you! Hang on... I still have to thank a man who I know extremely well and yet who remains a complete stranger – wandering happily around the garden centres and shopping arcades of a Sheffield which doesn't quite exist, for it is all in my head, or is it his head? Anyway, thanks John... Oof, you're welcome, Graham!